The Enchiridion

Of

Indulgences

NORMS AND GRANTS

Authorized English Edition
Issued by the Sacred Apostolic Penitentiary

CONTENTS

The Sacred Apostolic Penitentiary

Decree

In the Apostolic Constitution The Doctrine of Indulgences of January 1, 1967 we read: "Holy Mother Church has then deemed it fitting, in order to give greater dignity and esteem to the use of indulgences, to introduce some innovations into her discipline of indulgences and has accordingly ordered the issuance of new norms."

Norm 13 of the same Constitution decrees, moreover, as follows: "The Enchiridion of Indulgences [collection of indulgenced prayers and works] is to be revised with a view to attaching indulgences only to the most important prayers and works of piety, charity and penance."

In obedience to the will of the Sovereign Pontiff, as expressed both in the above-mentioned Apostolic Constitution and in further instructions from Him, this Sacred Penitentiary has seen to the careful preparation of a new Enchiridion of Indulgences.

The Sovereign Pontiff, Paul VI -- having received a report on the matter in an Audience granted on June 14 of the present year to the undersigned Cardinal, the Penitentiary Major -- on the 15th day of the same month approved, and ordered to be held authentic, the new Enchiridion of Indulgences as published by the Vatican Press. All general grants of indulgences, not included in this same Enchiridion, are hereby revoked. Revoked also are any ordinances concerning indulgences, not included in the Norms on Indulgences given below, whether in the Code of Canon Law, or in Apostolic Letters, even if issued "Motu proprio," or in Decrees of the Holy See.

Everything to the contrary notwithstanding, even if deserving of special mention.

Given at Rome, from the Sacred Apostolic Penitentiary, on the 29th day of June in the year 1968, the feast of the Holy Apostles, Peter and Paul.

† JOSEPH CARDINAL FERRETTO
Titular Bishop of the Suburban Church of Sabina and Poggio Mirteto
Penitentiary Major

John Sessolo Regent

Preliminary Observations

1. This new edition of the Enchiridion effectively implements Norm 13 of the Apostolic Constitution: "The Enchiridion of Indulgences is to be revised with a view to attaching indulgences only to the most important prayers and works of piety, charity and penance."

2. By the most important prayers and works are here meant those, which in the light of tradition and of the changed conditions of present times are indicated as particularly suited in helping the faithful to satisfy for the punishments due their sins and, what is of greater consequence still, in inciting them to a more fervent charity. It was with this principle in view, that the present new arrangement has been carried out. [1]

3. In accordance with traditional practice, participation in the Sacrifice of the Mass and in the Sacraments is not enriched with indulgences. This is because of the surpassing "sanctifying and purifying" [2] efficacy, which the Mass and the Sacraments have in themselves.

When, therefore, an indulgence is granted on certain special occasions (such as, first Holy Communion, the first Mass of a newly ordained priest, or the closing Mass of a Eucharistic Congress), it is to be understood as attached, not to the participation in the Mass or Sacraments as such, but to the extraordinary circumstances connected with the participation. Hence, what the indulgence is intended to promote and, so to speak, to reward are the personal devotion of the participant, which is the special aim of such celebrations, the giving of good example to others, and the manifestation of honor to the august mystery of the Eucharist and to the priesthood.

But an indulgence can be given, as is clear from tradition, to various works of private and public piety; likewise, works of charity and penance, which must be held as having even greater importance at the present time, can be so enriched. All these indulgenced works, however, as for that matter every other good work and every suffering patiently borne, are by no means to be esteemed apart from the Mass and the Sacraments, the principal sources of sanctification and purification; [3] for, it is precisely their good works and sufferings that constitute the oblation, which the faithful join to the oblation of Christ in the Eucharistic Sacrifice; [4] it is also the Mass and the Sacraments, which move the faithful to perform the tasks laid upon them in such a way that "they will hold fast in their lives to what they have received by faith"; [5] on the other hand, it is through the devoted fulfillment of their tasks, that they become daily ever better disposed to participate fruitfully in the Mass and Sacraments. [6]

4. In conformity with the changed conditions of present times, greater value is placed on the action (opus operantis) of the faithful. For this reason, instead of being a lengthy series of indulgenced works of piety (opus operatum), more or less extraneous to the daily life of the

---

[1] See Address of Pope Paul VI to College of Cardinals and to Roman Curia on Dec. 23, 1966: A.A.S., 59 (1967), p. 57.
[2] See Apost. Const. *The Doctrine of Indulgences*, Jan. 1, 1967, n. 11
[3] See Apost. Const. *The Doctrine of Indulgences*, n. 11
[4] See II Vatican Council, *Dogmatic Const. On the Church*, n. 34.
[5] Roman Missal, oration of Tuesday within octave of Easter.
[6] See II Vatican Council, *Const. On Sacred Liturgy*, nn. 9-13.

faithful, the number of indulgences now granted is relatively small. [7] By these it is hoped that the faithful will be more effectively moved to live holier and more useful lives, thus healing "the split between the faith which many profess and their daily lives . . . by gathering their humane, domestic, professional, social and technical enterprises into one vital synthesis with religious values, under whose supreme direction all things are harmonized unto God's glory." [8]

The new Enchiridion, therefore, is much shorter than what it was formerly. For certain prayers and pious works have been left out, while others have been brought under the general grants of indulgences.

The main concern has been to attach greater importance to a Christian way of life and to lead souls to cultivate the spirit of prayer and penance and to practice the theological virtues, rather than merely to repeat certain formulas and acts.

5. Before enumerating the various grants of indulgences, the Enchiridion contains a series of Norms, drawn from the norms of the Apostolic Constitution and from the canons of the Code of Canon Law still in force.

This procedure has been deemed advisable, both to anticipate any difficulties that might later arise and to provide at the same time an orderly and comprehensive exposition of the present discipline on Indulgences.

6. Three general grants of indulgences are first presented in the Enchiridion. These are intended to be a beacon, so to speak, to light the way of the faithful in their daily lives.

Included at times under these general grants are certain pious works, which were indulgenced in times past also.

For the benefit and instruction of the faithful, each of the general grants of indulgences is followed by various citations from the New Testament and from the documents of the II Vatican Council, the intent being to show the conformity of these grants with the spirit of the Gospel and with the renewal proposed by the Council.

7. The general grants of indulgences are followed by grants of indulgences attached to particular pious works. These are few in number, since works of this kind are provided for to a certain extent under the general grants of indulgences. In the matter of prayers, a selection has been made in favor of those which have a more universal appeal. Concerning other prayers, customarily used in particular rites and places, the competent ecclesiastical Authority can decide what is to be done.

8. An Appendix, containing a number of invocations, is added to the Enchiridion, which is then brought to a close with the text, included for documentation purposes, of the Apostolic Constitution The Doctrine of Indulgences.

_____

[7] See below, especially nn. I-III, pp. 33-40.
[8] See II Vatican Council, *Pastoral Const. On Church in the Modern World*, n. 43.

Norms On Indulgences

1. An indulgence is the remission before God of the temporal punishment due for sins already forgiven as far as their guilt is concerned. This remission the faithful with the proper dispositions and under certain determined conditions acquire through the intervention of the Church which, as minister of the Redemption, authoritatively dispenses and applies the treasury of the satisfaction won by Christ and the Saints. [1]

2. An indulgence is partial or plenary, according as it removes either part or all of the temporal punishment due for sin. [2]

3. No one, acquiring indulgences, can apply them to other living persons. [3]

4. Partial as well as plenary indulgences can always be applied to the departed by way of suffrage. [4]

5. The grant of a partial indulgence is designated only with the words "partial indulgence," without any determination of days or years. [5]

6. The faithful, who at least with contrite heart perform an action to which a partial indulgence is attached, obtain, in addition to the remission of temporal punishment acquired by the action itself, an equal remission of punishment through the intervention of the Church. [6]

7. The division of indulgences into "personal," "real" and "local" is abolished, so as to make it clearer that indulgences are attached to the actions of the faithful, even though at times they may be linked with some object or place. [7]

8. Besides the Roman Pontiff, to whom the dispensation of the whole spiritual treasury of the Church has been entrusted by Christ our Lord, they only can grant indulgences by ordinary power, to whom this is expressly conceded by law. [8]

9. In the Roman Curia, whatever pertains to the granting and use of indulgences is committed to the Sacred Penitentiary exclusively, saving the right of the Congregation for the Doctrine of the Faith to examine whatever pertains to dogmatic teaching concerning indulgences. [9]

10. No one below the Roman Pontiff can:

---

[1] N. 1 of *The Doctrine of Indulgences* (=norm 1 of Apostolic Const. *The Doctrine of Indulgences*: see section on Norms towards the end of this volume.)
[2] N. 2 of *The Doctrine of Indulgences*.
[3] See can. 930 of Code of Canon Law.
[4] N. 3 of *The Doctrine of Indulgences*.
[5] N. 4 of *The Doctrine of Indulgences*.
[6] N. 5 of *The Doctrine of Indulgences*.
[7] N. 12 of *The Doctrine of Indulgences*
[8] See can. 912 of Code of Canon Law.
[9] See Apost. Const. Regimini Ecclesiae Universae of Aug. 15, 1967, n. 113: A.A.S., 59 (1967), p. 923.

1° Give to others the faculty of granting indulgences, unless he has this right by express indult from the Apostolic See;

2° Add another indulgence to a work already indulgenced by the Apostolic See or by someone else, unless new conditions to be fulfilled are prescribed. [10]

11. Diocesan Bishops, and others equated to them in law, have the right from entrance upon their pastoral office:

§ 1. To grant a partial indulgence to persons or in places under their jurisdiction; [11a]

§ 2. To impart in their respective dioceses, according to the prescribed formula, the Papal Blessing with a plenary indulgence three times a year on solemn feasts of their own choice, even if they only assist at the solemn Mass. [11b]

12. Metropolitans can grant a partial indulgence in their suffragan Sees, as in their proper diocese. [12]

13. Patriarchs can grant a partial indulgence in each place, even if exempt, of their respective patriarchies, in churches of their rite outside the territory of their patriarchates, and to the faithful of their rite everywhere. Major Archbishops have the same faculty. [13]

14. Cardinals have the faculty of granting a partial indulgence in places or to institutes or persons under their jurisdiction or protection; in other places also, but only to persons present and for that time only. [14]

15. § 1. All books of indulgences, as well as pamphlets, leaflets and the like, whose contents include grants of indulgences, may not be published without the permission of the Ordinary or Hierarch of the place.

§ 2. The express permission of the Apostolic See is required to print and publish in any language the authentic collection of prayers and pious works, to which the Apostolic See has attached indulgences. [15]

16, Those who have asked and obtained from the Sovereign Pontiff grants of indulgences for all the faithful are obliged, under penalty of nullity of the favor thus obtained, to submit to the Sacred Penitentiary authentic copies of these same grants. [16]

---

[10] See can. 913 of Code of Canon Law.
[11a] See can. 349, § 2, 2° of Code of Canon Law; see Motu proprio *Cleri sanctitati* of June 2, 1957, can 396, § 2, 2°; can. 364, § 3, 3°; can, 367, § 2, 1° and can. 391: A.A.S., 49 (1957), pp. 541ff.
[11b] See can. 914 of Code of Canon Law; see also Motu proprio *Suburbicaritiis sedibus* of Apr. 11, 1962, II, 2: A.A.S., 54 (1962), p. 255.
[12] See can. 274 of Code of Canon Law; see Motu proprio *Cleri sanctitati,* can. 319, 6° and can. 320, § 1, 4°.
[13] See Motu proprio *Cleri sanctitati,* can. 283, 4°; see also can. 326, § 1, 10° (can 319, 6°) and § 2.
[14] See can. 239 of Code of Canon Law; see Motu proprio *Cleri sanctitati,* can. 185, § 1, 24°.
[15] See can. 1388 of Code of Canon Law.
[16] See can. 920 of Code of Canon Law.

17. If a feast or its external solemnity is legitimately transferred, it is understood that an indulgence, attached to the feast, is transferred to the same day. [17]

18. A visit to a church or oratory, if required to gain an indulgence attached to a certain day, can be made from noon of the preceding day to midnight at the close of the day itself. [18]

19. The faithful, who devoutly use an article of devotion (crucifix or cross, rosary, scapular or medal) properly blessed by any priest, obtain a partial indulgence. [19]

But if the article of devotion has been blessed by the Sovereign Pontiff or by any Bishop, the faithful, using it devoutly, can also gain a plenary indulgence on the feast of the Holy Apostles, Peter and Paul, provided they also make a profession of faith according to any legitimate formula.

20. § 1. Indulgences attached to a visit to a church do not cease if the church is totally destroyed, provided the church is rebuilt within fifty years in the same or almost the same place and under the same title.

§ 2. An indulgence attached to the use of an article of devotion only ceases, when the article is completely destroyed or is sold. [20]

21. Holy Mother Church, extremely solicitous for the faithful departed, has decided to apply suffrages to them as abundantly as possible in every Sacrifice of the Mass, abolishing every particular privilege in this regard. [21]

22. § 1. To be capable of gaining an indulgence for oneself, it is required that one be baptized, not excommunicated, in the state of grace at least at the completion of the prescribed works, and a subject of the one granting the indulgence.

§ 2. In order that one who is capable may actually gain indulgences, one must have at least a general intention to gain them and must in accordance with the tenor of the grant perform the enjoined works at the time and in the manner prescribed. [22]

23. Unless the tenor of the grant clearly indicates otherwise, indulgences granted by a Bishop can be gained by his subjects even outside his territory and by others within his territory who are exempt or who have or do not have a domicile elsewhere. [23]

24. § 1. A plenary indulgence can be acquired once only in the course of a day.

---

[17] See can. 922 of Code of Canon Law; see also Code of Rubrics, nn. 356-359: A.A.S., 52 (1960), p. 657.
[18] See can. 923 of Code of Canon Law.
[19] N. 17 of *The Doctrine of Indulgences.*
[20] See can. 924 of Code of Canon Law.
[21] N. 20 of *The Doctrine of Indulgences.*
[22] See can. 925 of Code of Canon Law; see can. 2262.
[23] See can. 927 of Code of Canon Law.

§ 2. But one can obtain the plenary indulgence for the moment of death, even if another plenary indulgence had already been acquired on the same day.

§ 3. A partial indulgence can be acquired more than once a day, unless otherwise expressly indicated. [24]

25. The work prescribed for acquiring a plenary indulgence connected with a church or oratory consists in a devout visit and the recitation during the visit of one Our Father and the Creed. [25]

26. To acquire a plenary indulgence it is necessary to perform the work to which the indulgence is attached and to fulfill the following three conditions: sacramental confession, eucharistic Communion, and prayer for the intention of the Sovereign Pontiff. It is further required that all attachment to sin, even venial sin. be absent.

If the latter disposition is in any way less than perfect or if the prescribed three conditions are not fulfilled, the indulgence will be partial only, saving the provisions given below in Norm 34 and in Norm 35 concerning those who are "impeded." [26]

27. The three conditions may be fulfilled several days before or after the performance of the prescribed work; it is, however, fitting that Communion be received and the prayer for the intention of the Sovereign Pontiff be said on the same day the work is performed. [27]

28. A single sacramental confession suffices for gaining several plenary indulgences; but Communion must be received and prayer for the intention of the Sovereign Pontiff must be recited for the gaining of each plenary indulgence. [28]

29. The condition of praying for the intention of the Sovereign Pontiff is fully satisfied by reciting one Our Father and one Hail Mary; nevertheless, each one is free to recite any other prayer according to his piety and devotion. [29]

30. The norms regarding plenary indulgences, particularly the one stated above in Norm 24, 1, apply also to what up to now have been customarily called "toties quoties" ["as often as"] plenary indulgences. [30]

31. An indulgence cannot be gained by a work, to which one is obliged by law or precept. unless the contrary is expressly stated in the grant; one, however, who performs a work which has been imposed as a sacramental penance and which happens to be one enriched with an indulgence, can at the same time both satisfy the penance and gain the indulgence. [31]

---

[24] N. 6 of *The Doctrine of Indulgences,* see also N. 18.
[25] N. 16 of *The Doctrine of Indulgences.*
[26] N. 7 of *The Doctrine of Indulgences.*
[27] N. 8 of *The Doctrine of Indulgences.*
[28] N. 9 of *The Doctrine of Indulgences.*
[29] N. 10 of *The Doctrine of Indulgences.*
[30] N. 19 of *The Doctrine of Indulgences.*
[31] See can. 932 of Code of Canon Law.

32. An indulgence attached to a prayer can be acquired by reciting the prayer in any language, provided the fidelity of the translation is vouched for by a declaration either of the Sacred Penitentiary or of any Ordinary or Hierarch of those places, where the language of the translation is the one commonly spoken. [32]

33. To gain an indulgence attached to a prayer, it is sufficient to recite the prayer alternately with a companion or to follow it mentally while it is being recited by another. [33]

34. Confessors can commute either the prescribed work or conditions, in favor of those who, because of a legitimate impediment, cannot perform the work or fulfill the conditions. [34]

35. Local Ordinaries or Hierarchs, moreover, can grant to the faithful, over whom they exercise legitimate authority and who live in places where it is impossible or at least very difficult to go to confession or Communion, permission to gain a plenary indulgence without confession and Communion, provided they have true contrition for their sins and have the intention of receiving these Sacraments as soon as possible. [35]

36. The deaf and dumb can gain indulgences attached to public prayers, if they devoutly raise their mind and affections to God, while others of the faithful are reciting the prayers in the same place; for private prayers it suffices, if they recite them mentally or with signs, or if they merely read them with their eyes. [36]

---

[32] See can. 934, § 2 of Code of Canon Law.
[33] See can. 934, § 3 of Code of Canon Law.
[34] See can. 935 of Code of Canon Law.
[35] N. 11 of *The Doctrine of Indulgences.*
[36] See can. 936 of Code of Canon Law.

Three General Grants Of Indulgences

Foreword

1. Presented in the first place are three grants of indulgences, intended to serve as a reminder to the faithful to infuse with the Christian spirit the actions that go to make up their daily lives [1] and to strive in the ordering of their lives toward the perfection of charity. [2]

2. The first and second grants are a resume of many given in times past; the third, on the other hand, is something altogether new but most suited to the present time when, with the mitigation of the law of fast and abstinence, it is more than ever imperative that penance be practiced in other ways. [3]

3. The three grants are truly general in character, each of them comprising many works of the same kind. However, not all such works are enriched with indulgences, but those only which are performed in a particular manner and spirit.

An example in point is the first grant, which reads as follows: "A partial indulgence is granted to the faithful who, in the performance of their duties and in bearing the trials of life, raise their mind with humble confidence to God, adding-even if only mentally -- some pious invocation."

By virtue of this grant those acts only are indulgenced, by which the faithful, while performing their duties and patiently suffering the trials of life, raise their mind to God in the manner indicated.

Acts of this kind, considering the frailty of human nature, are not frequent.

But should anyone be so zealous and fervent as to make such acts frequently in the course of a day, he would justly merit -- over and above a copious increase of grace -- a fuller remission of the punishment due for sin and he would in his charity be able to come to the aid of the souls in purgatory so much the more generously.

The above observations apply with practically the same force to the second and third grants.

4. The three grants are fully in harmony with the Gospel and with the teachings of the II Vatican Council. To illustrate this briefly for the benefit of the faithful, each of the three grants is followed by citations from the Sacred Scriptures and from the Acts of the Council.

---

[1] See 1 *Cor.* 10, 31 and *Col.* 3, 17; II Vatican Council, *Decree on the Apostolate of the Laity*, nn. 2, 3, 4, 13.
[2] See II Vatican Council, *Dogmatic Const. on the Church*, n. 39 and nn. 40-42.
[3] See Apost. Const. *Repent* of Feb. 17, 1966, III, c: A.A.S., 58 (1966), pp. 182-183.

I

First General Grant

A partial indulgence is granted to the faithful who, in the performance of their duties and in bearing the trials of life, raise their mind with humble confidence to God, adding even if only mentally -- some pious invocation.

This first grant is intended to serve as an incentive to the faithful to put into practice the commandment of Christ that "they must always pray and not lose heart" [4] and at the same time as a reminder so to perform their respective duties as to preserve and strengthen their union with Christ.

Mt 7, 7-8: Ask, and it shall be given you; seek, and you shall find; knock, and it shall be opened. For everyone who asks receives, and he who seeks finds, and to him who knocks it shall be opened.

Mt 26, 41: Watch and pray, that you may not enter into temptation.

Lk 21, 34-36: But take heed to yourselves, lest your hearts be overburdened ... with the cares of this life.... Watch, then, praying at all times.

Acts 2, 42: And they continued steadfastly in the teaching of the Apostles and in the communion of the breaking of the bread and in the prayers.

Rom 12, 12: Rejoicing in hope, . . . patient in tribulation, persevering in prayer.

1 Cor 10, 31: Therefore, whether you eat or drink, or do anything else, do all for the glory of God.

Eph 6, 18: With all prayer and supplication pray at all times in the Spirit, and therein be vigilant in all perseverance and supplication.

Col 3, 17: Whatever you do in word or in work, do all in the name of the Lord Jesus, giving thanks to God the Father through him.

Col 4, 2: Be assiduous in prayer, being wakeful therein with thanksgiving.

1 Thes 5, 17-18: Pray without ceasing. In all things give thanks.

II Vatican Council, Dogmatic Const. on the Church, n. 41: Finally, all Christ's faithful, whatever be the conditions, duties and circumstances of their lives -- and indeed through all these -- will daily increase in holiness, if they receive all things with faith from the hand of their heavenly Father and if they cooperate with the divine will. In this temporal service, they will manifest to all men the love with which God loved the world.

---

[4] *Lk 18, 1.*

II Vatican Council, Decree on the Apostolate of the Laity, n. 4: This life of intimate union with Christ in the Church is nourished by spiritual aids.... These are to be used by the laity in such a way that, while correctly fulfilling their secular duties in the ordinary conditions of life, they do not separate union with Christ from their life but rather performing their work according to God's will they grow in that union.... Neither family concerns nor other secular affairs should be irrelevant to their spiritual life, in keeping with the words of the Apostle, "Whatever you do in word or work, do all in the name of the Lord Jesus Christ, giving thanks to God the Father through him." [5]

II Vatican Council, Pastoral Const. on the Church in the Modern World, n. 43: This split between the faith which many profess and their daily lives deserves to be counted among the more serious errors of our age.... Therefore, let there be no false opposition between professional and social activities on the one hand, and religious life on the other.... Christians should rather rejoice that, following the example of Christ who worked as an artisan, they are free to give proper exercise to all their earthly activities and to their humane, domestic, professional, social and technical enterprises by gathering them into one vital synthesis with religious values, under whose supreme direction all things are harmonized unto God's glory.

II

Second General Grant

A partial indulgence is granted to the faithful, who in a spirit of faith and mercy give of themselves or of their goods to serve their brothers in need.

This second grant is intended to serve as an incentive to the faithful to perform more frequent acts of charity and mercy, thus following the example and obeying the command of Christ Jesus. [6]

However, not all works of charity are thus indulgenced, but only those which "serve their brothers in need," in need, for example, of food or clothing for the body or of instruction or comfort for the soul.

Mt 25, 35-36. 40: For I was hungry and you gave me to eat; I was thirsty and you gave me to drink; I was a stranger and you took me in; naked and you covered me; sick and you visited me; I was in prison and you came to me.... Amen I say to you, as long as you did it for one of these, the least of my brethren, you did it for me. [7]

Jn 13, 34-35: A new commandment I give you, that you love one another: that as I have loved you, you also love one another. By this will all men know that you are my disciples, if you have love for one another.

---

[5] *Col* 3, 17
[6] *Jn* 13, 15; *Acts* 10, 38.
[7] See also *Tb* 4, 7-8 and *Is* 58, 7.

Rom 12, 8. 10-11. 13: He who gives, in simplicity; . . . he who shows mercy, with cheerfulness.... Love one another with fraternal charity, anticipating one another with honor. Be not slothful in zeal; be fervent in spirit, serving the Lord.... Share the needs of the saints, practicing hospitality.

I Cor 13, 3: And if I distribute all my goods to feed the poor, . . . yet do not have charity, it profits me nothing.

Gal 6, 10: While we have time, let us do good to all men, but especially to those who are of the household of the faith.

Eph 5, 2: Walk in love, as Christ also loved us.

1 Thes 4, 9: You yourselves have learned from God to love one another.

Heb 13, 1: Let brotherly love abide in you.

Jas 1, 27: Religion pure and undefiled before God the Father is this: to give aid to orphans and widows in their tribulation and to keep oneself unspotted from this world. [8]

1 Pt 1, 22: Now that your obedience to charity has purified your souls for a brotherly love that is sincere, love one another heartily and intensely.

1 Pt 3, 8-9: Finally, be all like-minded, compassionate, lovers of the brethren, merciful, humble; not rendering evil for evil, or abuse for abuse, but contrariwise, blessing; for unto this were you called that you might inherit blessing.

2 Pt 1, 5. 7: Do you accordingly strive diligently to supply . . . your piety with fraternal love, your fraternal love with charity.

1 Jn 3, 17-18: He who has the goods of this world and sees his brother in need and closes his heart to him, how does the love of God abide in him? My dear children, let us not love in word, neither with the tongue, but in deed and in truth.

II Vatican Council, *Decree on the Apostolate of the Laity*, n. 8: Wherever there are people in need of food and drink, clothing, housing, medicine, employment, education; wherever men lack the facilities necessary for living a truly human life or are afflicted with serious distress or illness or suffer exile or imprisonment, there Christian charity should seek them out and find them, console them with great solicitude and help them with appropriate relief.... In order that the exercise of charity on this scale may be unexceptionable in appearance as well as in fact, it is altogether necessary to consider in one's neighbor the image of God in which he has been created, and also Christ the Lord to whom is really offered whatever is given to a needy person.

---

[8] See *Jas* 2, 15-16.

14

II Vatican Council, *Decree on the Apostolate of the Laity*, n. 31c: Since the works of charity and mercy express the most striking testimony of the Christian life, apostolic formation should lead also to the performance of these works so that the faithful may learn from childhood on to have compassion for their brethren and to be generous in helping those in need.

II Vatican Council, *Pastoral Const. on the Church in the Modern World*, n. 93: Mindful of the Lord's saying: "by this will all men know that you are my disciples, if you have love for one another,"[9] Christians cannot yearn for anything more ardently than to serve the men of the modern world with mounting generosity and success.... Now the Father wills that in all men we recognize Christ our brother and love him effectively in word and in deed.

III

Third General Grant

A partial indulgence is granted to the faithful, who in a spirit of penance voluntarily deprive themselves of what is licit and pleasing to them.

This third grant is intended to move the faithful to bridle their passions and thus learn to bring their bodies into subjection and to conform themselves to Christ in his poverty and suffering.[10]

But self-denial will be more precious, if it is united to charity, according to the teaching of St. Leo the Great: "Let us give to virtue what we refuse to self-indulgence. Let what we deny ourselves by fast -- be the refreshment of the poor."[11]

Lk 9, 23: If anyone wishes to come after me, let him deny himself, and take up his cross daily, and follow me.[12]

Lk 13, 5: Unless you repent, you will all perish in the same manner (see 13, 3).

Rom 8, 13: But if by the spirit you put to death the deeds of the flesh, you will live.

Rom 8, 17: Provided, however, we suffer with him that we may also be glorified with him.

1 Cor 9, 25-27: And everyone in a contest abstains from all things, and they indeed to receive a perishable crown, but we an imperishable. I, therefore, so run as not without a purpose; I so fight as not beating the air; but I chastise my body and bring it into subjection.

2 Cor 4, 10: Always bearing about in our body the dying of Jesus, so that the life also of Jesus may be made manifest in our bodily frame.

---

[9] *Jn* 13, 35.
[10] See *Mt* 8, 20 and 16, 24.
[11] Sermon 13, *On the Fast of the Tenth Month*, 2: PL 54, 172.
[12] See *Mt* 10, 30 and *Lk* 14, 27.

2 Tm 2, 11-12: This saying is true: If we have died with him, we shall also live with him; if we endure, we shall also reign with him.

Ti 2, 12: In order that rejecting . . . worldly lusts, we may live temperately and justly and piously in this world.

1 Pt 4, 13: Partakers of the sufferings of Christ, rejoice that you may also rejoice with exultation in the revelation of his glory.

II Vatican Council, Decree on Priestly Training, n. 9: With a particular concern should they be so formed in priestly obedience, in a simple way of life and in the spirit of self-denial that they are accustomed to give up willingly even those things that are permitted but are not expedient, and to conform themselves to Christ crucified.

II Vatican Council, Dogmatic Const. on the Church, n. 10: But the faithful, in virtue of their royal priesthood, join in the offering of the Eucharist. They likewise exercise that priesthood in receiving the sacraments, in prayer and thanksgiving, in the witness of a holy life, and by self-denial and active charity.

II Vatican Council, Dogmatic Const. on the Church, n. 41: In the various classes and differing duties of life, one and the same holiness is cultivated by all, who are moved by the Spirit of God and who obey the voice of the Father and worship God the Father in spirit and in truth. These people follow the poor Christ, the humble and crossbearing Christ, in order to be worthy of being sharers in his glory.

Apost. Const. Repent, III c: The Church urges all the faithful to live up to the divine commandment of penance by afflicting their bodies by some acts of chastisement, over and above the discomforts and annoyances of everyday life.... The Church wants to point out that there are three principal ways of satisfying the commandment to do penance, handed down from ancient times -- prayer, fasting and works of charity -- even though abstinence from meat and fasting have received special stress. These penitential methods could be found in all ages, but in our day there are special reasons why one method is encouraged more than the others because of local circumstances. Thus, in nations enjoying greater economic prosperity, encouragement should be given to offering some evidence of self-denial so that Christians will not conform to the world, and at the same time to offering some evidence of charity toward brothers, including those living far away, who are suffering from hunger and poverty.[13]

---

[13] A.A.S., 58 (1966), pp. 182-183.

Other Grants Of Indulgences

Foreword

1. To the three general grants of indulgences considered above under nn. I-III, a few others are here added. These it has seemed beneficial to include, either because of traditional esteem in the case of the old, or because appropriate to the needs of the present in the case of the new.

All these grants complement one another and, while by the offer of an indulgence they move the faithful to perform works of piety, charity and penance, they at the same time bring them into an ever closer union through charity with Christ the Head and with the Church his body. [1]

2. Certain prayers of venerable antiquity and in practically universal use have been retained from the previous edition of the Enchiridion of Indulgences, as for example, the Profession of Faith (n. 16), the psalm Out of the Depths (n. 19), the Magnificat (n. 30), the prayers We fly to your Patronage(n. 57), Hail, holy Queen (n. 51), Direct, we beg you, O Lord (n. 1), We give you thanks (n. 7).

On closer inspection it will be seen that many of these prayers come within the scope of the first of the three general grants, as for example, the prayers Direct, we beg you, Lord (n. 1) and We give you thanks (n. 7).

It has, however, been judged expedient to single them out as indulgenced prayers, for the twofold purpose of eliminating all doubt in this regard and of emphasizing their excellence.

3. Other prayers, formerly included in the *Enchiridion of Indulgences*, have been omitted, for the reason that they are prayers proper only to particular rites of the East or to particular regions of the West. The respective Patriarchs and Bishops of these rites and regions, moreover, can by using the faculties given them by law always indulgence these prayers, should they so wish.

4. Retained, moreover, from the previous edition of the *Enchiridion of Indulgences*, are certain works of greater importance, though somewhat changed where this was deemed appropriate.

5. The individual works, described in the following pages, are each enriched with indulgences. The grant of a partial indulgence is sometimes expressly stated; very often, however, it is merely indicated by the words: Partial indulgence.

If a particular work, when performed in special circumstances, is enriched with a plenary indulgence, this fact, as well as the special circumstances in which the work must be performed, are expressly noted each time; but other requirements for the gaining of a plenary indulgence are, for the sake of brevity, left understood.

---

[1] See Apost. Const. *The Doctrine of Indulgences,* n. 11.

As stated in Norm 26, the requirements for the gaining of a plenary indulgence are: the performance of the work, the fulfillment of the three conditions, and a disposition of mind and heart which totally excludes all affection to sin.

6. If the work, enriched with a plenary indulgence, can fittingly be divided into separate parts (for example, the decades of the *Marian Rosary*) and if for a reasonable cause it cannot be performed in its entirety, a partial indulgence can be gained for the part completed.

7. Deserving of special mention are the following works, for any one of which the faithful can gain a plenary indulgence each day of the year -- saving, however, the provision of Norm 24, § 1, according to which no one can gain more than one plenary indulgence in the course of a single day:

-- adoration of the Blessed Sacrament for at least one half an hour (n. 3);

-- devout reading of the Sacred Scriptures for at least one half an hour (n. 50);

-- the pious exercise of the Way of the Cross (n. 63);

-- the recitation of the Marian Rosary in a church or public oratory or in a family group, a religious Community or pious Association (n. 48).

The various grants of indulgences in the official Latin text of the Enchiridion are listed in alphabetical order. In the case of prayers, it is the first words of the prayer that determine its position in this arrangement (for example, Agimus tibi gratias - Angelus Domini); in the case of works, it is the first words by which the work is described (for example, Viae Crucis exercitium - Votorum baptismalium renovatio). *

---

* To obviate any confusion in citing the prayers and works of the Enchiridion by numerical reference, these prayers and works are given in the present English translation in the same order as in the official Latin text; for this reason the Latin designation of each prayer and work is given within parentheses beneath the English designation. (*Trans. note*)

INDULGENCED PRAYERS

1. Direct, we beg you, O Lord
(Actiones nostras)

Direct, we beg you, O Lord, our actions by your holy inspirations, and carry them on by your gracious assistance, that every prayer and work of ours may begin always with you, and through you be happily ended. Amen. (Roman Ritual

partial indulgence.

2. Acts of the Theological Virtues and of Contrition
(Actus virtutum theologalium et contritionis

A partial indulgence is granted to the faithful, who recite devoutly, according to any legitimate formula, the acts of the theological virtues (faith, hope, charity and of contrition .

Each act is indulgenced.

3. Adoration of the Most Blessed Sacrament
(Adoratio Ss.mi Sacramenti

A partial indulgence is granted to the faithful, who visit the Most Blessed Sacrament to adore it; a plenary indulgence is granted, if the visit lasts for at least one half an hour.

4. Hidden God
(Adoro te devote

Hidden God, devoutly I adore you,
Truly present underneath these veils:
All my heart subdues itself before you,
Since it all before you faints and fails.

Not to sight, or taste, or touch be credit,
Hearing only do we trust secure;
I believe, for God the Son has said it --
Word of Truth that ever shall endure.

On the cross was veiled your Godhead's splendor,
Here your manhood lies hidden too;
Unto both alike my faith I render,
And, as sued the contrite thief, I sue.

Though I look not on your wounds with Thomas,
You, my Lord, and you, my God, I call:
Make me more and more believe your promise,
Hope in you, and love you over all.

O memorial of my Savior dying,

Living Bread, that gives life to man;
Make my soul, its life from you supplying,
Taste your sweetness, as on earth it can.

Deign, O Jesus, Pelican of heaven,
Me, a sinner, in your Blood to lave,
To a single drop of which is given
All the world from all its sin to save.

Contemplating, Lord, your hidden presence,
Grant me what I thirst for and implore,
In the revelation of your essence
To behold your glory evermore.

A partial indulgence is granted to the faithful, who recite devoutly the above hymn.

5. We have come
(Adsumus)

We have come, O Lord, Holy Spirit, we have come before you, hampered indeed by our many and grievous sins, but for a special purpose gathered together in your name.

Come to us and be with us and enter our hearts.

Teach us what we are to do and where we ought to tend; show us what we must accomplish, in order that, with your help, we may be able to please you in all things.

May you alone be the author and the finisher of our judgments, who alone with God the Father and his Son possess a glorious name.

Do not allow us to disturb the order of justice, you who love equity above all things. Let not ignorance draw us into devious paths. Let not partiality sway our minds or respect of riches or persons pervert our judgment.

But unite us to you effectually by the gift of your grace alone, that we may be one in you and never forsake the truth; inasmuch as we are gathered together in your name, so may we in all things hold fast to justice tempered by mercy, so that in this life our judgment may in no wise be at variance with you and in the life to come we may attain to everlasting rewards for deeds well done. Amen. *(Roman Pontifical)*

This prayer, usually recited at the opening of a meeting to discuss matters of common interest, is enriched with a partial indulgence.

6. To you, O blessed Joseph
(Ad te, beate Joseph)

To you, O blessed Joseph, do we come in our tribulation, and having implored the help of your most holy spouse, we confidently invoke your patronage also. Through that charity which bound you to the immaculate Virgin Mother of God and through the paternal love with which you embraced the Child Jesus, we humbly beg you graciously to regard the inheritance which Jesus Christ has purchased by his Blood, and with your power and strength to aid us in our necessities.

O most watchful Guardian of the Holy Family, defend the chosen children of Jesus Christ; O most loving father, ward off from us every contagion of error and corrupting influence; O our most mighty protector, be propitious to us and from heaven assist us in our struggle with the power of darkness; and, as once you rescued the Child Jesus from deadly peril, so now protect God's Holy Church from the snares of the enemy and from all adversity; shield, too, each one of us by your constant protection, so that, supported by your example and your aid, we may be able to live piously, to die holily, and to obtain eternal happiness in heaven. Amen.

partial indulgence.

7. We give you thanks
(Agimus tibi gratias)

We give you thanks, Almighty God, for all your blessings: who live and reign for ever and ever. Amen. (Roman Breviary)

partial indulgence.

8. Angel of God
(Angele Dei)

Angel of God, my guardian dear, to whom his love commits me here, enlighten and guard, rule and guide me. Amen.

partial indulgence

9. The Angel of the Lord
(Angelus Domini)

a) During the year (outside of Paschal Season)

> V. The Angel of the Lord declared unto Mary,
> R. And she conceived of the Holy Spirit.
> Hail Mary.

> V. Behold the handmaid of the Lord,
> R. Be it done unto me according to your word.
> Hail Mary.

> V. And the Word was made flesh,

R. And dwelt among us.
Hail Mary.

V. Pray for us, O holy Mother of God,
R. That we may be made worthy of the promises of Christ.

Let us pray. Pour forth, we beg you, O Lord, your grace into our hearts: that we, to whom the Incarnation of Christ your Son was made known by the message of an Angel, may by his Passion and Cross be brought to the glory of his Resurrection. Through the same Christ our Lord. Amen.

b) During Paschal Season

Queen of Heaven, rejoice, alleluia:
For he whom you merited to bear, alleluia,
Has risen, as he said, alleluia.
Pray for us to God, alleluia.

V. Rejoice and be glad, O Virgin Mary, alleluia.
R. Because the Lord is truly risen, alleluia.

Let us pray. O God, who by the Resurrection of your Son, our Lord Jesus Christ, granted joy to the whole world: grant, we beg you, that through the intercession of the Virgin Mary, his Mother, we may lay hold of the joys of eternal life. Through the same Christ our Lord. Amen. (*Roman Breviary*)

A partial indulgence is granted to the faithful, who devoutly recite the above prayers according to the formula indicated for the time of the year.

It is a praiseworthy practice to recite these prayers in the early morning, at noon, and in the evening.

10. Soul of Christ
(Anima Christi)

Soul of Christ, sanctify me.
Body of Christ, save me.
Blood of Christ, inebriate me.
Water from the side of Christ, wash me.
Passion of Christ, strengthen me.
O good Jesus, hear me.
Within your wounds, hide me.
Separated from you let me never be.
From the malignant enemy, defend me.
At the hour of death, call me.
To come to you, bid me,
That I may praise you in the company

Of your Saints, for all eternity. Amen.

partial indulgence.

11. Visit to the Patriarchal Basilicas in Rome
(Basilicarum Patriarchalium in Urbe visitatio)

A plenary indulgence is granted to the faithful, who devoutly visit one of the four Patriarchal Basilicas in Rome, and there recite one *Our Father* and the *Creed.*

1) on the titular feast;
2) on any holy-day of obligation; [2]
3) once a year, on any other day of one's choice.

12. Papal Blessing
(Benedictio Papalis)

A plenary indulgence is granted to the faithful, who piously and devoutly receive, even by radio transmission, the Blessing of the Sovereign Pontiff, when imparted to Rome and the World.

13. Visit to a Cemetery
(Coemeterii visitatio)

An indulgence, applicable only to the Souls in Purgatory, is granted to the faithful, who devoutly visit a cemetery and pray, even if only mentally, for the departed. The indulgence is plenary each day from the 1st to the 8th of November; on other days of the year it is partial.

14. Visit to an early Christian Cemetery or 'catacomb'
(Coemeterii veterum christianorum seu 'catacumbae' visitatio)

A partial indulgence is granted to the faithful, who devoutly visit one of the early christian cemeteries or "'catacomb's."

15. Act of Spiritual Communion
(Communionis spiritualis actus)

An Act of Spiritual Communion, according to any pious formula, is enriched with a partial indulgence.

16. I believe in God
(Credo in Deum)

I believe in God, the Father Almighty, Creator of heaven and earth. And in Jesus Christ, his only Son, our Lord: who was conceived by the Holy Spirit, born of the Virgin Mary, suffered

---

[2] See can. 1247, § 1 of Code of Canon Law.

under Pontius Pilate, was crucified, died, and was buried; he descended into hell; the third day he rose again from the dead; he ascended into heaven; sitteth at the right hand of God the Father Almighty; from thence he shall come to judge the living and the dead. I believe in the Holy Spirit, the holy Catholic Church, the communion of Saints, the forgiveness of sins, the resurrection of the body, and life everlasting. Amen. (Apostles' Creed - Roman Ritual)

I believe in one God, the Father almighty, maker of heaven and earth, and of all things visible and invisible. And I believe in one Lord, Jesus Christ, the only-begotten Son of God. Born of the Father beyond all ages. God of God, Light of Light, true God of true God. Begotten, not made, of one substance with the Father. By whom all things were made. Who for us men and for our salvation came down from heaven. And he became flesh by the Holy Spirit of the Virgin Mary: and was made man. He was also crucified for us, suffered under Pontius Pilate, and was buried. And on the third day he rose again, according to the Scriptures. He ascended into heaven and sits at the right hand of the Father. He will come again in glory to judge the living and the dead. And of his kingdom there will be no end. And I believe in the Holy Spirit, the Lord and Giver of life, who proceeds from the Father and the Son. Who together with the Father and the Son is adored and glorified, and who spoke through the prophets. And one holy, Catholic, and Apostolic Church. I confess one baptism for the forgiveness of sins. And I await the resurrection of the dead. And the life of the world to come. Amen. (*Nicene-Constantinopolitan Creed - Roman Missal*)

A partial indulgence is granted to the faithful, who piously recite the Apostles' Creed or the Nicene-Constantinopolitan Creed.

17. Adoration of the Cross
(Crucis adoratio)

A plenary indulgence is granted to the faithful, who in the solemn liturgical action of Good Friday devoutly assist at the adoration of the Cross and kiss it.

18. Office of the Dead
(Defunctorum officium)

A partial indulgence is granted to the faithful, who devoutly recite Lauds or Vespers of the Office of the Dead.

19. Out of the Depths
(De profundis)

Out of the depths I cry to you, O Lord;
    Lord, hear my voice!
Let your ears be attentive
    to my voice in supplication:
If you, O Lord, mark iniquities,
    Lord, who can stand?
But with you is forgiveness,
    that you may be revered.

I trust in the Lord;
   my soul trusts in his word.
My soul waits for the Lord,
   more than sentinels wait for the dawn.
More than sentinels wait for the dawn,
   let Israel wait for the Lord;
For with the Lord is kindness
   and with him is plenteous redemption;
And he will redeem Israel from all their iniquities.

A partial indulgence is granted to the faithful, who piously recite the psalm Out of the depths (Ps 129).

20. Christian Doctrine
(Doctrina christiana)

A partial indulgence is granted to the faithful, who take part in teaching or in learning christian doctrine. N.B.: One who in a spirit of faith and charity teaches christian doctrine can gain a partial indulgence according to the second of the three general grants of indulgences; see above (p. 35). This new grant confirms the partial indulgence in favor of the teacher of christian doctrine and extends it to the learner.

21. Lord God Almighty
(Domine, Deus omnipotens)

Lord, God Almighty, you have brought us safely to the beginning of this day. Defend us today by your mighty power, that we may not fall into any sin, but that all our words may so proceed and all our thoughts and actions be so directed, as to be always just in your sight. Through Christ our Lord. Amen. (Roman Breviary)

partial indulgence.

22. Look down upon me, good and gentle Jesus
(En ego, o bone et dulcissime Iesu)

Look down upon me, good and gentle Jesus, while before your face I humbly kneel, and with burning soul pray and beseech you to fix deep in my heart lively sentiments of faith, hope and charity, true contrition for my sins, and a firm purpose of amendment, while I contemplate with great love and tender pity your five wounds, pondering over them within me, calling to mind the words which David, your prophet, said of you, my good Jesus: "They have pierced my hands and my feet; they have numbered all my bones" (Ps 21, 17-18).

A plenary indulgence is granted on each Friday of Lent and Passiontide to the faithful, who after Communion piously recite the above prayer before an image of Christ crucified; on other days of the year the indulgence is partial.

23. Eucharistic Congress

(Eucharisticus conventus)

A plenary indulgence is granted to the faithful, who devoutly participate in the customary solemn eucharistic rite at the close of a Eucharistic Congress.

24. Hear us
(Exaudi nos)

Hear us, Lord, holy Father, almighty and eternal God; and graciously send your holy angel from heaven to watch over, to cherish, to protect, to abide with, and to defend all who dwell in this house. Through Christ our Lord. Amen. (Roman Ritual)

partial indulgence.

25. Spiritual Exercises
(Exercitia spiritualia)

A plenary indulgence is granted to the faithful, who spend at least three whole days in the spiritual exercises of a retreat.

26. Most sweet Jesus -- Act of Reparation
(Iesu dulcissime - Reparationis actus)

Most sweet Jesus, whose overflowing charity for men is requited by so much forgetfulness, negligence and contempt, behold us prostrate before you, eager to repair by a special act of homage the cruel indifference and injuries to which your loving Heart is everywhere subject.

Mindful, alas! that we ourselves have had a share in such great indignities, which we now deplore from the depths of our hearts, we humbly ask your pardon and declare our readiness to atone by voluntary expiation, not only for our own personal offenses, but also for the sins of those, who, straying far from the path of salvation, refuse in their obstinate infidelity to follow you, their Shepherd and Leader, or, renouncing the promises of their baptism, have cast off the sweet yoke of your law.

We are now resolved to expiate each and every deplorable outrage committed against you; we are now determined to make amends for the manifold offenses against Christian modesty in unbecoming dress and behavior, for all the foul seductions laid to ensnare the feet of the innocent, for the frequent violations of Sundays and holy-days, and the shocking blasphemies uttered against you and your Saints. We wish also to make amends for the insults to which your Vicar on earth and your priests are subjected, for the profanation, by conscious neglect or terrible acts of sacrilege, of the very Sacrament of your divine love, and lastly for the public crimes of nations who resist the rights and teaching authority of the Church which you have founded.

Would that we were able to wash away such abominations with our blood. We now offer, in reparation for these violations of your divine honor, the satisfaction you once made to your Eternal Father on the cross and which you continue to renew daily on our altars; we offer it in union with the acts of atonement of your Virgin Mother and all the Saints and of the pious faithful on earth; and we sincerely promise to make recompense, as far as we can with the help of your grace, for all neglect of your great love and for the sins we and others have committed in the past. Henceforth, we will live a life of unswerving faith, of purity of conduct, of perfect observance of the precepts of the Gospel and especially that of charity. We promise to the best of our power to prevent others from offending you and to bring as many as possible to follow you.

O loving Jesus, through the intercession of the Blessed Virgin Mother, our model in reparation, deign to receive the voluntary offering we make of this act of expiation; and by the crowning gift of perseverance keep us faithful unto death in our duty and the allegiance we owe to you, so that we may all one day come to that happy home, where with the Father and the Holy Spirit you live and reign, God, forever and ever. Amen.

A partial indulgence is granted to the faithful, who piously recite the above act of reparation. A plenary indulgence is granted if it is publicly recited on he feast of the Most Sacred Heart of Jesus.

27. Most sweet Jesus, Redeemer -- Act of Dedication of the Human Race to Jesus Christ King
(Iesu dulcissime, Redemptor)

Most sweet Jesus, Redeemer of the human race, look down upon us humbly prostrate before you. We are yours, and yours we wish to be; but to be more surely united with you, behold each one of us freely consecrates himself today to your Most Sacred Heart. Many indeed have never known you; many, too, despising your precepts, have rejected you. Have mercy on them all, most merciful Jesus, and draw them to your Sacred Heart. Be King, O Lord, not only of the faithful who have never forsaken you, but also of the prodigal children who have abandoned you; grant that they may quickly return to their Father's house, lest they die of wretchedness and hunger. Be King of those who are deceived by erroneous opinions, or whom discord keeps aloof, and call them back to the harbor of truth and the unity of faith, so that soon there may be but one flock and one Shepherd. Grant, O Lord, to your Church assurance of freedom and immunity from harm; give tranquility of order to all nations; make the earth resound from pole to pole with one cry: Praise to the divine Heart that wrought our salvation; to it be glory and honor for ever. Amen.

A partial indulgence is granted to the faithful, who piously recite the above Act of Dedication of the Human Race to Jesus Christ King. A plenary indulgence is granted, if it is recite publicly on the feast of our Lord Jesus Christ King.

28. The Moment of Death
(In articulo mortis)

To the faithful in danger of death, who cannot be assisted by a priest to bring them the sacraments and impart the Apostolic Blessing with its plenary indulgence (see can. 468, 2 of Code of Canon Law), Holy Mother Church nevertheless grants a plenary indulgence to be acquired at the point of death, provided they are properly disposed and have been in the habit of reciting some prayers during their lifetime. The use of a crucifix or a cross to gain this indulgence is praiseworthy.

The condition: provided they have been in the habit of reciting some prayers during their lifetime supplies in such cases for the three usual conditions required for the gaining of a plenary indulgence.

The plenary indulgence at the point of death can be acquired by the faithful, even if they have already obtained another plenary indulgence on the same day.

The above grant is taken from the Apostolic Constitution The Doctrine of Indulgences, Norm 18.

29. Litanies
(Litaniae)

The following Litanies are each enriched with a partial indulgence:

the Most Holy Name of Jesus,
the Most Sacred Heart of Jesus,
the Most Precious Blood of Jesus,
the Blessed Virgin Mary,
St. Joseph,
All Saints.

30. Magnificat
(Magnificat)

My soul magnifies the Lord,
    and my spirit rejoices in God my Savior;
Because he has regarded the lowliness of his handmaid;
    for, behold, henceforth all generations shall call me blessed;
Because he who is mighty has done great things for me,
    and holy is his name;
And his mercy is from generation to generation
    on those who fear him.
He has shown might with his arm,
    he has scattered the proud in the conceit of their heart.
He has put down the mighty from their thrones,
    and has exalted the lowly.
He has filled the hungry with good things,
    and the rich he has sent away empty.
He has given help to Israel, his servant,
    mindful of his mercy --
Even as he spoke to our fathers --
    to Abraham and to his posterity forever.

A partial indulgence is granted to the faithful, who piously recite the canticle of the Magnificat.

31. Mary, Mother of Grace
(Maria, Mater gratiae)

Mary, Mother of grace, Mother of mercy, Shield me from the enemy And receive me at the hour of my death. (Roman Ritual)

partial indulgence.

32. Remember, O most gracious Virgin Mary
(Memorare, o piissima Virgo Maria)

Remember, O most gracious Virgin Mary, that never was it known that anyone who fled to your protection, implored your help or sought your intercession, was left unaided. Inspired with this confidence, I fly to you, O Virgin of virgins, my Mother; to you do I come, before you I stand, sinful and sorrowful. O Mother of the Word Incarnate, despise not my petitions, but in your mercy hear and answer me. Amen.

partial indulgence.

33. Have mercy on me
(Miserere)

Have mercy on me, O God, in your goodness;
in the greatness of your compassion wipe out my offense.
Thoroughly wash me from my guilt
and of my sin cleanse me.

For I acknowledge my offense,
    and my sin is before me always:
"Against you only have I sinned,
    and done what is evil in your sight,"
That you may be justified in your sentence,
    vindicated when you condemn.
Indeed, in guilt was I born,
    and in sin my mother conceived me;
Behold, you are pleased with sincerity of heart,
    and in my inmost being you teach me wisdom.

Cleanse me of sin with hyssop, that I may be purified;
    wash me, and I shall be whiter than snow.
Let me hear the sounds of joy and gladness;
    the bones you have crushed shall rejoice.
Turn away your face from my sins,
    and blot out all my guilt.

A clean heart create for me, O God,
    and a steadfast spirit renew within me.
Cast me not out from your presence,
    and your holy spirit take not from me.
Give me back the joy of your salvation,
    and a willing spirit sustain in me.

I will teach transgressors your ways,
    and sinners shall return to you.
Free me from blood guilt, O Lord, my saving God;
    then my tongue shall revel in your justice.
O Lord, open my lips,
    and my mouth shall proclaim your praise.
For you are not pleased with sacrifices;
    should I offer a holocaust, you would not accept it.
My sacrifice, O God, is a contrite spirit;
    a heart contrite and humbled, O God, you will not spurn.

Be bountiful, O Lord, to Sion in your kindness
    by rebuilding the walls of Jerusalem;
Then shall you be pleased with due sacrifices,
    burnt offerings and holocausts; then shall they offer up bullocks on your altar.

A partial indulgence is granted to the faithful, who with repentant heart recite the psalm Have mercy on me (Ps 50).

34. Novena Devotions
(Novendiales preces)

A partial indulgence is granted to the faithful, who devoutly take part in the pious exercises of a public novena before the feast of Christmas or Pentecost or the Immaculate Conception of the Blessed Virgin Mary.

35. Use of Articles of Devotion
(Obiectorum pietatis usus)

The faithful, who devoutly use an article of devotion (crucifix or cross, rosary. scapular or medal) properly blessed by any priest, [3] obtain a partial indulgence.

---

[3] In order to bless an article or devotion properly the priest uses the prescribed fromula, if there is any; otherwise, he makes a simple sign of the cross toward the article of devotion, laudably adding the words: "In the name of the Father, and of the Son, and of the Holy Spriti".

In practice, a formula is to be used in the public blessing of scapulars, while a sign of the cross suffices for other cases.

But if the article of devotion has been blessed by the Sovereign Pontiff or by any Bishop, the faithful, using it, can also gain a plenary indulgence on the feast of the Holy Apostles, Peter and Paul, provided they also make a profession of faith according to any legitimate formula.

The above grant is taken from the Apostolic Constitution The Doctrine of Indulgences, *Norm 17*. See above, *Norm 19*.

36. Little Offices
(Officia parva)

The following Little Offices are each enriched with a partial indulgence:

the Passion of our Lord Jesus Christ,
the Most Sacred Heart of Jesus,
the Immaculate Conception of the Blessed Virgin Mary,
St. Joseph.

37. Prayer for Sacerdotal or Religious Vocations
(Oratio ad sacerdotales vel religiosas vocationes impetrandas)

A partial indulgence is granted to the faithful, who recite a prayer, approved by ecclesiastical Authority, for the above intention

38. Mental Prayer
(Oratio mentalis)

A partial indulgence is granted to the faithful, who piously spend some time in mental prayer.

39. Let us pray for our Sovereign Pontiff
(Oremus pro Pontifice)

V. Let us pray for our Sovereign Pontiff N.
R. The Lord preserve him and give him life, and make him blessed upon the earth, and deliver him not up to the will of his enemies. (*Roman Breviary*)

partial indulgence.

40. O Sacred Banquet
(O sacrum convivium)

O sacred banquet, in which Christ is received, the memory of his Passion is renewed, the mind is filled with grace, and a pledge of future glory is given to us. (Roman Breviary)

partial indulgence.

41 Assistance at Sacred Preaching
(Praedicationis sacrae participatio)

A partial indulgence is granted to the faithful, who assist with devotion and attention at the sacred preaching of the Word of God.

A plenary indulgence is granted to the faithful, who during the time of a Mission have heard some of the sermons and are present for the solemn close of the Mission.

42. First Communion
(Prima Communio)

A plenary indulgence is granted to the faithful, when they receive Communion for the first time, or when they assist at the sacred ceremonies of a First Communion.

43. First Mass of newly-ordained Priests
(Prima Missa neosacerdotum)

A plenary indulgence is granted to a priest on the occasion of the first Mass he celebrates with some solemnity and to the faithful who devoutly assist at the same Mass.

44. Prayer for Unity of the Church
(Pro unitate Ecclesiae oratio)

Almighty and merciful God, you willed that the different nations should become one people through your Son. Grant in your kindness that those, who glory in being known as Christians, may put aside their differences and become one in truth and charity, and that all men, enlightened by the true faith, may be united in fraternal communion in the one Church. Through Christ our Lord. Amen.

partial indulgence.

45. Monthly Recollection
(Recollectio menstrua)

A partial indulgence is granted to the faithful, who take part in a monthly retreat.

46 Eternal Rest
(Requiem aeternam)

Eternal rest grant to them, O Lord, and let perpetual light shine upon them. May they rest in peace. (Roman Breviary)

partial indulgence, applicable only to the souls in purgatory.

47 May it please you, O Lord
(Retribuere dignare, Domine)

May it please you, O Lord, to reward with eternal life all those who do good to us for your Name's sake. Amen. (Roman Breviary

partial indulgence.

48. Recitation of the Marian Rosary
(Rosarii marialis recitatio)

A plenary indulgence is granted, if the Rosary is recited in a church or public oratory or in a family group, a religious Community or pious Association; a partial indulgence is granted in other circumstances.

"Now the Rosary is a certain formula of prayer, which is made up of fifteen decades of "Hail Marys" with an "Our Father" before each decade, and in which the recitation of each decade is accompanied by pious meditation on a particular mystery of our Redemption." (Roman Breviary) The name "Rosary," however, is commonly used in reference to only a third part of the fifteen decades.

The gaining of the plenary indulgence is regulated by the following norms:

1) The recitation of a third part only of the Rosary suffices; but the five decades must be recited continuously.

2) The vocal recitation must be accompanied by pious meditation on the mysteries.

3) In public recitation the mysteries must be announced in the manner customary in the place; for private recitation, however, it suffices if the vocal recitation is accompanied by meditation on the mysteries.

4) For those belonging to the Oriental rites, amongst whom this devotion is not practiced, the Patriarchs can determine some other prayers in honor of the Blessed Virgin Mary (for those of the Byzantine rite, for example, the Hymn "Akathistos" or the Office "Paraclisis"); to the prayers thus determined are accorded the same indulgences as for the Rosary

49. Jubilees of Sacerdotal Ordination
(Sacerdotalis Ordinationis celebrationes iubilares)

A plenary indulgence is granted to a priest, who on the 25th, 50th and 60th anniversary of his Ordination renews before God his resolve to fulfill faithfully the duties of his vocation. If the priest celebrates a jubilee Mass in some solemn manner, the faithful, who assist at it, can acquire a plenary indulgence.

50. Reading of Sacred Scripture
(Sacrae Scripturae lectio)

A partial indulgence is granted to the faithful, who with the veneration due the divine word make a spiritual reading from Sacred Scripture. A plenary indulgence is granted, if this reading is continued for at least one half an hour.

51. Hail, holy Queen
(Salve, Regina)

Hail, holy Queen, Mother of mercy; hail our life, our sweetness and our hope. To you do we cry, poor banished children of Eve. To you do we send up our sighs, mourning and weeping in this valley of tears. Turn then, most gracious Advocate, your eyes of mercy toward us. And after this our exile show unto us the blessed fruit of your womb, Jesus. O clement, O loving, O sweet Virgin Mary. (Roman Breviary)

partial indulgence.

52. Holy Mary, help the helpless
(Sancta Maria, succurre miseris)

Holy Mary, help the helpless, strengthen the fearful, comfort the sorrowful, pray for the people, plead for the clergy, intercede for all women consecrated to God; may all who keep your sacred commemoration experience the might of your assistance. (Roman Breviary)

partial indulgence.

53. Holy Apostles Peter and Paul
(Sancti Apostoli Petre et Paule)

Holy Apostles Peter and Paul, intercede for us.

Guard your people, who rely on the patronage of your apostles Peter and Paul, O Lord, and keep them under your continual protection. Through Christ our Lord. Amen. (Roman Missal)

partial indulgence.

54. Veneration of the Saints
(Sanctorum cultus)

A partial indulgence is granted to the faithful, who on the feast of any Saint recite in his honor the oration of the Missal or any other approved by legitimate Authority.

55. Sign of the Cross
(Signum crucis)

A partial indulgence is granted to the faithful, who devoutly sign themselves with the sign of the cross, while saying the customary words: In the name of the Father, and of the Son, and of the Holy Spirit. Amen.

56. A Visit to the Stational Churches of Rome
(Stationalium Ecclesiarum Urbis visitatio)

A partial indulgence is granted to the faithful, who on the day indicated in the Roman Missal devoutly visit the Stational Church of Rome named for that day; but if they also assist at the sacred functions celebrated in the morning or evening, a plenary indulgence is granted.

57. We fly to your Patronage
(Sub tuum praesidium)

We fly to your patronage, O holy Mother of God; despise not our petitions in our necessities, but deliver us always from all dangers, O glorious and blessed Virgin. partial indulgence.

58. Diocesan Synod
(Synodus dioecesana)

A plenary indulgence is granted to the faithful, who during the time of the diocesan Synod devoutly visit the church, in which the Synod is being held, and there recite one Our Father and the Creed.

59. Down in adoration falling
(Tantum ergo)

Down in adoration falling,
Lo! the sacred Host we hail;
Lo! o'er ancient forms departing,
Newer rites of grace prevail;
Faith for all defects supplying,
Where the feeble senses fail.

To the everlasting Father,
And the Son who reigns on high,
With the Holy Spirit proceeding
Forth from each eternally,
Be salvation, honor, blessing,
Might and endless majesty. Amen.

V. You have given them bread from heaven,
R. Having all sweetness within it.

Let us pray. O God, who in this wonderful Sacrament left us a memorial of your Passion: grant, we implore you, that we may so venerate the sacred mysteries of your Body and Blood, as always to be conscious of the fruit of your Redemption. You who live and reign forever and ever. Amen. (Roman Breviary)

A partial indulgence is granted to the faithful, who devoutly recite the above strophes. But a plenary indulgence is granted on Holy Thursday and on the feast of Corpus Christi, if they are recited in a solemn manner.

60 The Te Deum
(Te Deum)

O God, we praise you, and acknowledge you to be the supreme Lord.
Everlasting Father, all the earth worships you.
All the Angels, the heavens and all angelic powers,
All the Cherubim and Seraphim, continuously cry to you:
Holy, holy, holy, Lord, God of Hosts!
Heaven and earth are full of the Majesty of your glory.
The glorious choir of the Apostles,
The wonderful company of Prophets,
The white-robed army of Martyrs, praise you.
Holy Church throughout the world acknowledges you:
The Father of infinite Majesty;
Your adorable, true and only Son;
Also the Holy Spirit, the Comforter.
O Christ, you are the King of glory!
You are the everlasting Son of the Father.
When you took it upon yourself to deliver man,
You did not disdain the Virgin's womb.
Having overcome the sting of death,
    you opened the Kingdom of Heaven to all believers.
You sit at the right hand of God in the glory of the Father.
We believe that you will come to be our Judge.
We, therefore, beg you to help your servants whom you have
    redeemed with your Precious Blood.
Let them be numbered with your Saints in everlasting glory.
Save your people, O Lord, and bless your inheritance!
Govern them, and raise them up forever.
Every day we thank you.
And we praise your Name forever; yes, forever and ever.
O Lord, deign to keep us from sin this day.
Have mercy on us, O Lord, have mercy on us.
Let your mercy, O Lord, be upon us, for we have hoped in you.
O Lord, in you I have put my trust; let me never be put to shame.

A partial indulgence is granted to the faithful, who recite the Te Deum in thanksgiving. But a plenary indulgence is granted, if the hymn is recited publicly on the last day of the year.

61. Come, Holy Spirit, Creator blest
(Veni, Creator)

Come, Holy Spirit, Creator blest,

And in our souls take up your rest;
Come with your grace and heavenly aid
To fill the hearts which you have made.

O Comforter, to you we cry,
O heavenly gift of God Most High,
O fount of life and fire of love,
And sweet anointing from above.

You in your sevenfold gifts are known;
You, finger of God's hand we own;
You, promise of the Father, you
Who do the tongue with power imbue.

Kindle our senses from above,
And make our hearts o'erflow with love;
With patience firm and virtue high
The weakness of our flesh supply.

Far from us drive the foe we dread,
And grant us your peace instead;
So shall we not, with you for guide,
Turn from the path of life aside.

Oh, may your grace on us bestow
The Father and the Son to know;
And you, through endless times confessed,
Of both the eternal Spirit blest.

Now to the Father and the Son,
Who rose from death, be glory given,
With you, O holy Comforter,
Henceforth by all in earth and heaven. Amen.

A partial indulgence is granted to the faithful, who devoutly recite the hymn Come, Holy
Spirit, Creator blest. But a plenary indulgence is granted, if the hymn is recited publicly on the
1st of January and on the feast of Pentecost.

62. Come, Holy Spirit
(Veni, Sancte Spiritus)

Come, Holy Spirit, fill the hearts of your faithful and enkindle in them the fire of your love.
(Roman Missal)

partial indulgence.

63. Exercise of the Way of the Cross

(Viae Crucis exercitium)

A plenary indulgence is granted to the faithful, who make the pious exercise of the Way of the Cross.

In the pious exercise of the Way of the Cross we recall anew the sufferings, which the divine Redeemer endured, while going from the praetorium of Pilate, where he was condemned to death, to the mount of Calvary, where he died on the cross for our salvation.

The gaining of the plenary indulgence is regulated by the following norms: ;

1) The pious exercise must be made before stations of the Way of the Cross legitimately erected.

2) For the erection of the Way of the Cross fourteen crosses are required, to which it is customary to add fourteen pictures or images, which represent the stations of Jerusalem.

3) According to the more common practice, the pious exercise consists of fourteen pious readings, to which some vocal prayers are added. However, nothing more is required than a pious meditation on the Passion and Death of the Lord, which need not be a particular consideration of the individual mysteries of the stations.
4) A movement from one station to the next is required.

But if the pious exercise is made publicly and if it is not possible for all taking part to go in an orderly way from station to station, it suffices if at least the one conducting the exercise goes from station to station, the others remaining in their place.

Those who are "impeded" can gain the same indulgence, if they spend at least one half an hour in pious reading and meditation on the Passion and Death of our Lord Jesus Christ.

For those belonging to Oriental rites, amongst whom this pious exercise is not practiced, the respective Patriarchs can determine some other pious exercise in memory of the Passion and Death of our Lord Jesus Christ for the gaining of this indulgence.

64. Visit, we beg you, O Lord
(Visita, quaesumus, Domine)

Visit, we beg you, O Lord, this dwelling, and drive from it all snares of the enemy: let your holy Angels dwell herein, to keep us in peace; and let your blessing be always upon us. Through Christ our Lord. Amen. (Roman Breviary)

partial indulgence.

65. Visit to the Parochial Church
(Visitatio ecclesiae paroecialis)

A plenary indulgence is granted to the faithful, who devoutly visit the parochial church:

-- on the titular feast;
-- on the 2nd of August, when the indulgence of the "Portiuncula" occurs.

Both indulgences can be acquired either on the day designated above or on some other day designated by the Ordinary for the benefit of the faithful.

The same indulgences apply to the Cathedral church and, where there is one, to a Co-Cathedral church, even if they are not parochial churches; they apply to quasi-parochial churches also. [4]

The above indulgences are contained in the Apostolic Constitution The Doctrine of Indulgences, Norm 15, with account being taken at the same time of proposals made to the Sacred Penitentiary in the meanwhile.

In visiting the church, it is required, according to Norm 16 of the same Apostolic Constitution, [5] that "one Our Father and the Creed be recited."

66. Visit to a Church or an Altar on the day of its consecration
(Visitatio ecclesiae vel altaris die consecrationis)

A plenary indulgence is granted to the faithful, who visit a church or an altar on the day itself of its consecration, and there recite one Our Father and the Creed.

67 Visit to a Church or Oratory on All Souls Day
(Visitatio ecclesiae vel oratorii in Commemoratione omnium fidelium defunctorum)

A plenary indulgence, applicable only to the Souls in Purgatory, is granted to the faithful, who on the day dedicated to the Commemoration of all the faithful departed piously visit a church, a public oratory or -- for those entitled to use it -- a semipublic oratory.

The above indulgence can be acquired either on the day designated above or, with the consent of the Ordinary, on the preceding or following Sunday or the feast of All Saints.

The above indulgence is contained in the Apostolic Constitution The Doctrine of Indulgences, Norm 15, with account being taken of proposals made to the Sacred Penitentiary in the meantime.

In visiting the church or oratory, it is required, according to Norm 16 of the same Apostolic Constitution, [6] that "one Our Father and the Creed be recited."

68. Visit to a Church or Oratory of Religious on the Feast of the Holy Founder
(Visitatio ecclesiae vel oratorii Religiosorum die festo Sancti Fundatoris)

---

[4] See can. 216, § 3 of Code of Canon Law.
[5] See also Norm 25 (p.25) above.
[6] See also Norm 25 (p.25) above.

A plenary indulgence is granted to the faithful, who devoutly visit a church or oratory of Religious on the Feast of the canonized Founder, and there recite one Our Father and the Creed.

69. Pastoral Visitation
(Visitatio pastoralis)

A partial indulgence is granted to the faithful, who devoutly visit a church or a public or semipublic oratory during the time that a pastoral visitation is being held; but a plenary indulgence, to be gained once only, is granted, if during the time of the visitation they assist at a sacred function at which the Visitator presides. [7]

70. Renewal of Baptismal Promises
(Votorum baptismalium renovatio)

A partial indulgence is granted to the faithful, who renew their baptismal promises according to any formula in use; but a plenary indulgence is granted, if this is done in the celebration of the Paschal Vigil or on the anniversary of one's baptism.

---

[7] See can. 343, 315, 274, n.5, 301, § 2 of Code of Canon Law.

Appendix : Pious Invocations

In regard to any invocation, the following observations are to be noted:

1) An invocation, as far as indulgences are concerned, is no longer considered a work, distinct and complete in itself, but as complementing an action, by which the faithful raise their heart and mind with humble confidence to God in performing their duties or bearing the trials of life. Hence, a pious invocation perfects the inward elevation; both together are as a precious jewel joined to one's ordinary actions to adorn them, as salt added to them to season them properly.

2) That invocation is to be preferred which is best suited to the particular situation and one's personal dispositions, whether it is one that comes spontaneously to mind or is chosen from those approved through long-standing use by the faithful and brought together in the following brief list.

3) An invocation can be of the briefest kind, expressed in one or few words or only thought of mentally.

The following are cited by way of example: My God -- Father [1] -- Jesus -- May Jesus Christ be praised (or some similar customary christian greeting) -- Lord, I believe in you -- I adore you -- I place my trust in you -- I love you -- All for you -- I thank you (or Thanks be to God) -- May God be blessed (or Let us bless the Lord) -- Your kingdom come -- Your will be done -- As the Lord wills [2] -- O God, help me -- Comfort me -- Graciously hear me (or Hear my prayer -- Save me -- Have mercy on me -- O Lord, spare me -- Do not permit me to be separated from you -- Do not abandon me -- Hail, Mary -- Glory to God in the highest -- Great are you, O Lord. [3]

Examples of Invocations in Customary Use [4]

1) We adore you, O Christ, and we bless you; because by your holy Cross you have redeemed the world. (Roman Breviary)

2) May the Holy Trinity be blessed. (Roman Missal)

3) Christ conquers! Christ reigns! Christ commands!

4) O Heart of Jesus, burning with love for us, inflame our hearts with love for you.

5) O Heart of Jesus, I place my trust in you.

---

[1] See *Rom* 8, 15 and *Gal* 4, 6.
[2] See *Job* 1, 21.
[3] *Jdt* 15, 16; see *Ps* 85, 10.
[4] Other invocations, as expressed in the vernacular, may be found in commonly used prayer-books. For example, in English, My Jesus, mercy (proposed by St. Leonard of Port Maurice); Virgin Mary, Mother of God, make us saints (proposed by St. Joseph Cafasso).

6) O Heart of Jesus, all for you.

7) Most Sacred Heart of Jesus, have mercy on us.

8) My God and my all.

9) O God, have mercy on me, a sinner (Lk 18, 13).

10) Grant that I may praise you, O sacred Virgin; give me strength against your enemies. (Roman Breviary)

11) Teach me to do your will, because you are my God (Ps 142, 10).

12) O Lord, increase our faith (Lk 17, 5).

13) O Lord, may we be of one mind in truth and of one heart in charity.

14) O Lord, save us, we are perishing (Mt 8, 25).

15) My Lord and my God (Jn 20, 28).

16) Sweet Heart of Mary, be my salvation.

17) Glory be to the Father, and to the Son, and to the Holy Spirit. (Roman Missal)

18) Jesus, Mary, Joseph.

19) Jesus, Mary, Joseph, I give you my heart and my soul. Jesus, Mary, Joseph, assist me in my last agony. Jesus, Mary, Joseph, may I sleep and rest in peace with you. (Roman Ritual)

20) Jesus, meek and humble of heart, make my heart like your Heart. (Roman Ritual)

21) May the Most Blessed Sacrament be praised and adored forever.

22) Stay with us, O Lord (Lk 24, 29).

23) Mother of Sorrows, pray for us.

24) My Mother, my Hope.

25) Send, O Lord, laborers into your harvest (see Mt 9, 38).

26) May the Virgin Mary together with her loving Child bless us. (Roman Breviary)

27) Hail, O Cross, our only hope. (Roman Breviary)

28) All you holy men and women of God, intercede for us. (Roman Ritual)

29) Pray for us, O Holy Mother of God, that we may be made worthy of the promises of Christ. (Roman Ritual)

30) Father, into your hands I commend my spirit (Lk. 23, 46; see Ps 30, 6).

31) Merciful Lord Jesus, grant them everlasting rest. (Roman Missal)

32) Queen conceived without original sin, pray for us. (Roman Ritual)

33) Holy Mother of God, Mary ever Virgin, intercede for us. (Roman Breviary)

34) Holy Mary, pray for us. (Roman Ritual)

35) You are the Christ, the Son of the living God (Mt 16, 16).

Apostolic Constitution

The Doctrine Of Indulgences *

PAUL BISHOP

SERVANT OF THE SERVANTS OF GOD
FOR EVERLASTING REMEMBRANCE

I

1. The doctrine and practice of indulgences which have been in force for many centuries in the Catholic Church have a solid foundation in divine revelation [1] which comes from the Apostles and "develops in the Church with the help of the Holy Spirit," while "as the centuries succeed one another the Church constantly moves forward toward the fullness of divine truth until the words of God reach their complete fulfillment in her." [2]

For an exact understanding of this doctrine and beneficial use it is necessary, however, to remember truths which the entire Church illumined by the Word of God has always believed and which the bishops, the successors of the Apostles, and first and foremost among them the Roman Pontiffs, the successors of Peter, have taught by means of pastoral practice as well as doctrinal documents throughout the course of centuries to this day.

2. It is a divinely revealed truth that sins bring punishments inflicted by God's sanctity and justice. These must be expiated either on this earth through the sorrows, miseries and calamities of this life and above all through death, [3] or else in the life beyond through fire and

---

* The text (not the footnotes) of the Constitution is taken from the booklet published by the United States Catholic Conference.

[1] See Council of Trent, Session XXV, *Decree on Indulgences:* "Since the power of granting indulgences was bestowed by Christ on the Church and since, even in the earliest times, the Church made use of this power given to her by God . . .": D.S. (= Denzinger-Schoenmetzer) 1835; see. *Mt* 28. 18.

[2] II Vatican Council, Dogmatic Constitution on Divine Revelation, n. 8: A.A.S., 58 (1966), p. 821; see I Vatican Council, Dogmatic Constitution on the Catholic Faith., ch. 4 On Faith and Reason: D.S. 3020.

[3] See Gn 3, 16-19: "To the woman [God] said: 'I will make great your distress in child-bearing; in pain shall you bring forth children; for your husband shall be your longing, though he have dominion over you.' And to Adam he said: 'Because you have listened to your wife, and have eaten of the tree of which I commanded you not to eat: Cursed be the ground because of you; in toil shall you eat of it all the days of your life; thorns and thistles shall It bring forth to you.... In the sweat of your brow you shall eat bread, till you return to the ground, since out of it you were taken; for dust you are and unto dust you shall return.'"

See also *Lk* 19, 41-44; *Rom* 2, 9 and 1 *Cor* 11, 30.

See Augustine, *Exposition on Ps 58, 1, 13:* "Every sin, whether small or great, must be punished, either by man himself doing penance, or by God chastising him": CCL *39, p. 739; PL 36, 701.*

torments or "purifying" punishments. [4] Therefore it has always been the conviction of the faithful that the paths of evil are fraught with many stumbling blocks and bring adversities, bitterness and harm to those who follow them. [5]

These punishments are imposed by the just and merciful judgment of God for the purification of souls, the defense of the sanctity of the moral order and the restoration of the glory of God to its full majesty. Every sin in fact causes a perturbation in the universal order established by God in his ineffable wisdom and infinite charity, and the destruction of immense values with respect to the sinner himself and to the human community. Christians throughout history have always regarded sin not only as a transgression of divine law but also --though not always in a direct and evident way-- as contempt for or disregard of the friendship between God and man, [6] just as they have regarded it as a real and unfathomable offense against God and indeed an ungrateful rejection of the love of God shown us through Jesus Christ, who called his disciples friends and not servants. [7]

3. It is therefore necessary for the full remission and--as it is called--reparation of sins not only that friendship with God be reestablished by a sincere conversion of the mind and amends made for the offense against his wisdom and goodness, but also that all the personal as well as social values and those of universal order itself, which have been diminished or destroyed by sin, be fully reintegrated whether through voluntary reparation which will

---

See Thomas, S. Th. *1-2*, q. 87, a. 1: "And because sin is an inordinate act, It Is evident that whoever sins commits an offense against an order; wherefore he is put down, in consequence, by that same order. This repression is punishment."

[4] See *Mt* 25, 41-42: "Depart from me, accursed ones, into the everlasting fire which was prepared for the devil and his angels. For I was hungry and you did not give me to eat." See also *Mk* 9, 42-43; *Jn* 5, 28-29; *Rom* 2, 9; *Gal* 6, 6-8.

See II Council of Lyons, Session IV, *Profession of Faith of Emperor Michael Palaeologus: D.S. 856-858.*

See Council of Florence, *Decree for the Greeks: D.S. 1304-1306.*

See Augustine, *Enchiridion*, 66, 17: "Many sins, likewise, seem now to be overlooked and visited with no punishments, but the penalties for these are reserved for the time to come; for it is not in vain that that day is called the day of judgment in which the Judge of the living and the dead is to come. On the other hand, sins are punished now and will, provided they are pardoned, inflict no harm in the life to come. Accordingly, concerning certain temporal punishments inflicted on sinners in this life, the Apostle, referring to those whose sins have been blotted out and not reserved for the final Judgment, says (1 *Cor* 11, 31-32): 'For if we Judged ourselves, we would not be judged by the Lord; but when we are judged, we are being chastised by the Lord, that we may not be condemned with the world'": ed. Scheel, Tubingen 1930, p. 42; PL 40, 263.

[5] See The Shepherd of Hermas, Mand. 6, 1, 3: Funk, Apostolic Fathers 1, p. 487.
[6] See *Is* 1, 2-3: "Sons have I raised and reared, but they have disowned me. An ox knows its owner, and an ass, its master's manger. But Israel does not know, my people has not understood." See also *Dt* 8, 11 and 32, 15 ff ; *Ps* 105, 21 and *118, passim; Wis 7,* 14; *Is 17,* 10 and 44, 21; Jer 33, *8; Ez 20, 27.*

See II Vatican Council, *Dogmatic Constitution on Divine Revelation,* n. 2: "Through this revelation, therefore, the invisible God (see Col 1. 15; *1 Tm 1, 17*) out of the abundance of his charity speaks to men as friends (see Ex 33, 11; Jn 15, 14-15) and dwells with them (see *Bar* 3, 38), in order that he may invite and receive them into fellowship with himself": A.A.S., 58 (1966), P. 818. See also *same Const., n. 21: l.c. pp. 827-828.*
[7] See *Jn* 15, 14-15.

See II Vatican Council, Pastoral Constitution on the Church in the Modem World, n. 22: A.A.S., 58 (1966), p. 1042; Decree on the Missionary Activity of the Church, n. 13: A.A.S., 58 (1966), p. 962.

involve punishment or through acceptance of the punishments established by the just and most holy wisdom of God, from which there will shine forth throughout the world the sanctity and the splendor of his glory. The very existence and the gravity of the punishment enable us to understand the foolishness and malice of sin and its harmful consequences.

That punishment or the vestiges of sin may remain to be expiated or cleansed and that they in fact frequently do even after the remission of guilt [8] is clearly demonstrated by the doctrine on purgatory. In purgatory, in fact, the souls of those "who died in the charity of God and truly repentant, but before satisfying with worthy fruits of penance for sins committed and for omissions" [9] are cleansed after death with purgatorial punishments. This is also clearly evidenced in the liturgical prayers with which the Christian community admitted to Holy Communion has addressed God since most ancient times: "We are being justly punished for our sins, but be merciful and free us for the glory of your name." [10]

For all men who walk this earth daily commit at least venial sins; [11] thus all need the mercy of God to be set free from the penal consequences of sin.

---

[8] See *Nm* 20, 12: "But the Lord said to Moses and Aaron: 'Because you were not faithful to me in showing forth my sanctity before the Israelites, You shall not lead this community into the land I shall give them.'"

See *Nm* 27, 13-14: "When you have viewed it, you too shall be taken to your people, as was your brother Aaron, because in the rebellion of the community in the desert of Sin you both rebelled against my order to manifest my sanctity to them by means of the water."

See *2 Sm* 12, 13-14: "And David said to Nathan: 'I have sinned against the Lord., And Nathan said to David: 'The Lord also has taken away your sin; you shall not die. Nevertheless, because you have given occasion to the enemies of the Lord to blaspheme, for this thing the child, that is born to you, shall surely die.'"

See Innocent IV, *Instruction for the Greeks: D.S. 838.*

See Council of Trent, Session VI, can. 30: "If anyone should say that, after having received the grace of justification, the guilt of the repentant sinner and his debt of eternal punishment are so cancelled that no debt of temporal punishment remains, to be satisfied, before he can enter into the kingdom of heaven, either in this life or in the life to come in purgatory: let him be anathema": D.S. 1580; see also D.S. 1689, 1693.

See Augustine, *Tract on the Gospel of John,* 124, 5: "Man is obliged to suffer (in this life), even when his sins are forgiven, although it was the first sin that caused his falling into this misery. For the penalty is of longer duration than the guilt, lest the guilt should be accounted small, were the penalty also to end with it- It is for this reason--either to make manifest the indebtedness of his misery, or to correct his frailty in this life, or to exercise him in necessary patience-that man is held in this life to the penalty, even when he is no longer held to the guilt unto eternal damnation": CCL 36, pp. 683-684; PL 35, 1972-1973.

[9] II Council of Lyons, Session IV: D.S. 856.

[10] See *Roman Missal,* Prayer for Septuagesima Sunday: "O Lord, in your kindness hear the prayers of your people. We are being justly punished for our sins, but be merciful and free us for the glory of your name."

See *Roman Missal,* Prayer over the People for Monday after first Sunday in Lent: "Free us from the slavery of our sins, 0 Lord, and mercifully shield us from the punishments these sins deserve."

See *Roman Missal,* Prayer after Communion for third Sunday in Lent: "0 God, you have allowed us to share in this great sacrament. In your mercy free us also from all guilt and danger of sin."

[11] See *Jas* 3, 2: "For in many things we all offend."

II

4. There reigns among men, by the hidden and benign mystery of the divine will, a supernatural solidarity whereby the sin of one harms the others just as the holiness of one also benefits the others. [12] Thus the Christian faithful give each other mutual aid to attain their supernatural aim. A testimony of this solidarity is manifested in Adam himself, whose sin is passed on through propagation to all men. But of this supernatural solidarity the greatest and most perfect principle, foundation and example is Christ himself to communion with whom God has called us. [13]

5. Indeed Christ, "who committed no sin," "suffered for us," [14] "was wounded for our iniquities, bruised for our sins ... by his bruises we are healed." [15]

Following in the footsteps of Christ, [16] the Christian faithful have always endeavored to help one another on the path leading to the heavenly Father through prayer, the exchange of

---

See I *Jn* 1, 8: "If we say that we have no sin, we deceive ourselves, and the truth is not in us." The Council of Carthage comments on this text, as follows: "In regard to the words of the Apostle St. John: 'If we say that we have no sin, we deceive ourselves, and the truth is not in us,' the Council agreed to the following declaration: whoever should hold that this [text] is to be so understood as to mean that it is out of humility that we should say 'we have sin,' and not because this is truly so, let him be anathema": D.S. 228.

See Council of Trent, Session VI, *Decree on Justification,* ch 11: D.S. 1537.

See II Vatican Council, *Dogmatic Constitution on the Church,* n. 40: "But since we all offend in many things (see Jas 3, 2), we at stand in need of God's mercy continuously and must daily pray: 'And forgive us our trespasses' (Mt 6, 12) 11: A.A.S., 57 (1965), p. 45.

[12] See Augustine, *On Baptism, Against the Donatists,* 1, 28: PL 43, 124.

[13] See *Jn* 15, 5: "I am the vine, you are the branches. He who abides in me, and I in him, he bears much fruit."

See 1 Cor 12, 27; "Now you are the body of Christ, member for member." See also 1 *Cor 1,* 9 and 10, 17; *Eph 1,* 20-23 and 4, 4.

See II Vatican Council, *Dogmatic Constitution on the Church,* n. 7: A.A.S., 57 (1965), pp. 10-11.

See Pius *XII, Encyclical on the Mystical Body:* "Through this communication of the Spirit of Christ ... the Church becomes the fulness and complement of the Redeemer, Christ being in a certain sense filled out through the Church in all things (see Thomas, *Commentary an the Epistle to the Ephesians,* 1, lesson 8). In these words we arrive at the reason, why. . . the mystical Head, which is Christ, and the Church, which on this earth as another Christ bears his person, are the one new man, in whom heaven and earth are joined together in perpetuating the saving work of the Cross: by Christ we mean the Head and the Body, the whole Christ": D.S. 3813; A.A.S., 35 (1943), pp. 230-231.

See Augustine, *Exposition 2 an Ps 90, 1:* "Our Lord Jesus Christ, as a man complete and perfect, has both head and body. the head we acknowledge to be he who was born of the Virgin Mary. ... This head is the head of the Church. The body of this head is, not that Church which is in this place, but which is in this place and throughout the whole world: not that Church which exists at this time, but that which is made up of the Saints from Abel down to the last men to be born and to believe in Christ, all of them constituting one people and belonging to one city. It is this city which is the body, whose head is Christ": CCL 39, p. 1266; PL 37. 1159.

[14] See 1 *Pt* 2, 22 and 21.

[15] See Is 53, 4-6 and I *Pt* 2, 21-25; see also *Jn* 1, 29; *Rom* 4, 25 and 5, 9 ff I *Cor* 15, 3; 2 *Cor* 5, 21; *Gal* 1, 4; *Eph* 1, 7 ff ; *Heb* 1, 3. etc.; 1 *Jn* 3. 5.

spiritual goods and penitential expiation. The more they have been immersed in the fervor of charity, the more they have imitated Christ in his sufferings, carrying their crosses in expiation for their own sins and those of others, certain that they could help their brothers to obtain salvation from God the Father of mercies. [17] This is the very ancient dogma of the Communion of the Saints, [18] whereby the life of each individual son of God in Christ and through Christ is joined by a wonderful link to the life of all his other Christian brothers in the

---

[16] See 1 Pt 2, 21.

[17] See *Col* 1, 24: "I rejoice now in the sufferings I bear for your sake; and what is lacking of the suffering of Christ I fill up in my flesh for his body, which is the Church."

See Clement of Alexandria, *What Rich Man Shall Be Saved* 42: The Apostle St. john exhorts the youthful robber to repentance, exlaiming: "I suffer death for you, just as the Lord suffered death for us. I shall give my life vicariously for yours: GCS *Clement* 3, p. 190; PG 9, 650.

See Cyprian, On *Apostates* 17; 36: "We believe indeed that the merits of the martyrs and the works of the just can avail very much with the judge, when the day of judgment arrives and when this era and world come to an end and the people of Christ are standing before his tribunal." "To him who is repentant, who performs good works, who prays, he can be merciful and forgiving; he can regard as received from them, whatever the martyrs have asked and the priests done on their behalf": *CSEL 3* 1, pp. 249-250 and 263; *PL* 49 495 and 508.

See Jerome, *Against Vigilantius 6:* "*You* say in your booklet that we can pray one for another while we live, but that no one's prayer for another will be heard after we have died, especially since the martyrs, though crying out for the avenging of their blood, were not able to obtain it *(Ap 6, 10).* If the apostles and martyrs can pray for others while they are still in the flesh and while they must still have a care for themselves, how much more after they have been crowned, victorious and triumphant?": *PL* 23, 359.

See Basil the Great, *Homily on Julitta the Martyr* 9: "We must therefore weep with those who weep. When you see a brother mourning out of sorrow for his sins, weep with such a man and be sorrowful with him. For the sins of another will thus enable you to correct your own. For he, who sheds fervid tears for the sin of a neighbor, brings healing to himself, at the same time that he weeps for this brother. . . . Mourn because of sin. Sin is a sickness of the soul; it brings death to the immortal soul; sin deserves to be mourned and to be lamented with ceaseless weeping": PG 319 258-259.

See John Chrysostom, *Homily on the Epistle to the Philippians 1,* 39 3: "Let us not, therefore, mourn as a rule those who die, nor let us rejoice as a rule over those who live. What then? Let us mourn for sinners, not only when they die, but also while they live. Let us rejoice for the Just, not only while they live, but also after they have died": PG 62, 203.

See Thomas, S. *Th.* 1-2, q. 87, a. 8: "If we speak of that satisfactory punishment, which one takes upon oneself voluntarily, one may bear another's punishment, in so far as they are, in some way, one. . . . If, however, we speak of punishment inflicted on account of sin, inasmuch as it is penal, then each one is punished for his own sin only, because the sinful act is something personal. But if we speak of a punishment that is medicinal, in this way it does happen that one is punished for another's sin. For It has been stated that ills sustained in bodily goods or even in the body itself, are medicinal punishments intended for the health of the soul. Wherefore there is no reason why one should not have suchlike *punishments in*flicted on one for another's sin, either by God or by man."

[18] See Leo XIII, *Encyclical Mirae Caritatis:* "For the Communion of Saints is nothing other . . . than the mutual sharing of help, expiation, prayers and benefits among the faithful who, whether they are already in possession of their heavenly fatherland or are detained in Purgatory or are still living as pilgrims upon earth, are united and form one commonwealth, whose head is Christ, whose form is charity": *Acts of Leo XIII 22* (1902), p. 129; D.S. 3363.

supernatural unity of the Mystical Body of Christ till, as it were, a single mystical person is formed. [19]

Thus is explained the 'treasury of the Church" [20] which should certainly not be imagined as the sum total of material goods accumulated in the course of the centuries, but the infinite and inexhaustible value the expiation and the merits of Christ our Lord have before God, offered as they were so that all of mankind could be set free from sin and attain communion with the Father. It is Christ the Redeemer himself in whom the satisfactions and merits of his redemption exist and find their force. [21] This treasury also includes the truly immense, unfathomable and ever pristine value before God of the prayers and good works of the Blessed Virgin Mary and all the saints, who following in the footsteps of Christ the Lord and by his grace have sanctified their lives and fulfilled the mission entrusted to them by the Father. Thus while attaining their own salvation, they have also cooperated in the salvation of their brothers in the unity of the Mystical Body.

"For all who are in Christ, having his spirit, form one Church and cleave together in him" (Eph 4, 16). Therefore the union of the wayfarers with the brethren who have gone to sleep in the peace of Christ is not in the least weakened or interrupted, but on the contrary, according to the perpetual faith of the Church, is strengthened by a communication of spiritual goods. For by reason of the fact that those in heaven are more closely united with Christ, they establish the whole Church more firmly in holiness, lend nobility to the worship which the Church offers to God here on earth and in many ways contribute to building it up evermore (1 Cor 12, 12-27). For after they have been received into their heavenly home and are present to the Lord (2 Cor 5, 8), through him and with him and in him they do not cease to intervene with the Father for us, showing forth the merits which they have won on earth through the one

---

[19] See I *Cor* 12, 12-13: "For as the body is one and has many members, and all the members of the body, many as they are, form one body, so also is it with Christ. For in one Spirit we were all baptized into one body."

See Pius XII, *Encyclical on the Mystical Body:* "In a certain sense [Christ] so lives in the Church that it is as it were another Christ. The doctor of the Gentiles in his letter to the Corinthians affirms this when, without further qualification, he calls the Church 'Christ' (see I *Cor* 12, 12), following no doubt the example of his Master who called out to him from on high. 'Saul, Saul, why do you persecute me?' (see *Acts* 9. 4; 22, 7; *26, 14).* Indeed, if we are to believe Gregory of Nyssa, the Church is often called 'Christ' by the Apostle (see *The Life of Moses: PG 44,* 385); and you are conversant, Venerable Brothers, with that phrase of Augustine: 'Christ preaches Christ' (see *Sermons 354, 1; PL* 39, *1563) ":* A.A.S., 35 (1943), p. 218.

See Thomas, S. *Th. 3,* q. 48, a. 2, 1 and q. 49, a. 1.

[20] See Clement VI, Jubilee Bull The *Only-begotten Son of God:* "The only-begotten Son of God . . . acquired a treasure for the Church militant . . . This treasure . . . he bequeathed to the faithful, to be dispensed for their salvation by the blessed Peter, the keeper of the keys of heaven, and by his successors, the vicars of Christ on earth . . . . The riches of this treasure, as all acknowledge, are still further increased by the merits of the Blessed Mother of God and by the merits of all the elect from the first just man to the last . . .11: *D.S. 1025, 1026, 1027.*

See Sixtus IV, Encyclical *Romani Pontificis:* " . . . We, to whom the fullness of power has been given from on high, desirous of helping and assisting the souls in Purgatory from the treasury of, the universal Church,which is made up of the merits of Christ and of his Saints and which has been entrusted to Us . . .": D.S. 1406.

See Leo X, Decree *Cum postquam* to Cajetan de Vio, the Papal Legate: ". . . to dispense the treasure of the merits of Jesus Christ and of the Saints . . .": D.S. 1448; see D.S. 1467 and 2641.
[21] See *Heb* 7, 23-25; 9, 11-28.

Mediator between God and man, Jesus Christ (1 Tim 2, 5), by serving God in all things and filling up in their flesh those things which are lacking of the sufferings of Christ for his Body which is the Church (Col 1, 24). Thus by their brotherly interest our weakness is greatly strengthened. [22]

For this reason there certainly exists between the faithful who have already reached their heavenly home, those who are expiating their sins in purgatory and those who are still pilgrims on earth a perennial link of charity and an abundant exchange of all the goods by which, with the expiation of all the sins of the entire Mystical Body, divine justice is placated. God's mercy is thus led to forgiveness, so that sincerely repentant sinners may participate as soon as possible in the full enjoyment of the benefits of the family of God.

III

6. The Church, aware of these truths ever since its origins, formulated and undertook various ways of applying the fruits of the Lord's redemption to the individual faithful and of leading them to cooperate in the salvation of their brothers, so that the entire body of the Church might be prepared in justice and sanctity for the complete realization of the kingdom of God, when he will be all things to all men.

The Apostles themselves, in fact, exhorted their disciples to pray for the salvation of sinners. [23] This very ancient usage of the Church has blessedly persevered, [24] particularly in the practice of penitents invoking the intercession of the entire community, [25] and when the dead are assisted with suffrages, particularly through the offering of the Eucharistic Sacrifice. [26]

---

[22] See II Vatican Council, *Dogmatic Constitution on the Church*, n. 49. A.A.S., 57 (1965), pp. 54-55.

[23] See *Jas* 5, 16: "Confess, therefore, your sins to one another, and pray for one another, that you may be saved. For the unceasing prayer of a just man is of great avail."

See 1 *Jn* 5, 16: "He who knows his brother is committing a sin that is not unto death, let him ask and life shall be given to him who does not commit a sin unto death."

[24] See Clement of Rome, *To the Corinthians* 56, 1: "Let us also therefore pray for those who are in sin of any kind, that they may be granted the self-mastery and humility to submit, not to us, but to the divine win. For thus the commendation of them to God and the Saints, which is accompanied by mercy, will be fruitful for them and perfect": Funk, *The Apostolic Fathers 1, p. 171.*

See *Martyrdom of St. Polycarp* 8, 1: "But when at last he finished his prayer, in which he made mention of all who at one time or other had been associated with him and who included the small and the great, the famous and the unknown, and the whole catholic church throughout the world . . .": Funk, *Apostolic Fathers* 1, p. 321, 323.

[25] See Sozomenus, *History of the Church* 7, 16: In public penance, after the celebration of Mass, the penitents in the Church of Rome "lamenting and weeping cast themselves prone on the ground. Then the Bishop with tears in his eyes comes toward them and prostrates likewise on the ground, the whole assembly of the faithful at the same time weeping and confessing their sins. The Bishop, thereupon, is the first to rise, bids the others to rise also, says an appropriate prayer for the sinners doing penance, and dismisses them": *PG* 67, 1462.

[26] See Cyril of Jerusalem, *Catechesis* 23 (mystag. 5), 9; 10: "We then pray also for our deceased holy fathers and bishops, and in general for an among us who departed this life, believing as we do that those souls, for whom prayer is offered, while the sacred and most venerable victim lies before us, will be most greatly helped." After illustrating this by the example of the wreath woven for the emperor that he may grant amnesty to those *in* exile, the holy Doctor concludes his discourse, saying: *"In* the same way we also, when we offer prayers to God for the departed, even if they are sinners, do not merely weave a wreath, but we present to God Christ Victimized for our sins, striving to obtain from his mercy favor and propitiation both for them and for ourselves": *PG* 33, 1115, 1118.

Good works, particularly those which human frailty finds difficult, were also offered to God for the salvation of sinners from the Church's most ancient times. [27] And since the sufferings of the martyrs for the faith and for the law of God were considered of great value, penitents used to turn to the martyrs, to be helped by their merits to obtain from the bishops a more speedy reconciliation. [28] Indeed the prayer and good works of the upright were considered to be of so great value that it could be asserted the penitent was washed, cleansed and redeemed with the help of the entire Christian people. [29]

It was not believed, however, that the individual faithful by their own merits alone worked for the remission of sins of their brothers, but that the entire Church as a single body united to Christ its Head was bringing about satisfaction. [30]

The Church of the Fathers was fully convinced that it was pursuing the work of salvation in community, and under the authority of the pastors established by the Holy Spirit as bishops to govern the Church of God. [31] The bishops, therefore, prudently assessing these matters, established the manner and the measure of the satisfaction to be made and indeed permitted canonical penances to be replaced by other possibly easier works, which would be useful to

---

See Augustine, *Confessions 9*, 12, 32: *PL 32, 777;* and 9, 11, *27: PL 32,* 775; *Sermons* 172, 2: *PL 38, 936;* Care *To Be Shown for the Dead 1, 3; PL 40, 593.*

[27] See Clement of Alexandria, *What Rich Man Shall Be Saved 42:* (About the Apostle St. John's conversion of the youthful robber) "From then on he spared no effort until-now by frequent prayers to God, now by joining with the youth in protracted fasts, now by persuasive and winning words-he succeeded in converting him to the Church with firm constancy . . .": *CGS 17, pp. 189-190; PG 9,* 651.

[28] See Tertullian, *To the Martyrs 1,* 6: "Some, not having this peace In the church, were wont to ask for it from the martyrs in prison": *CCL 1, p. 3; PL 1, 695.*

See Cyprian, *Epistle 18* (alias: *12), 1: "1* think we should come to the aid of our brethren who have received certificates from the martyrs, so that . . . , having received the imposition of hands unto repentance, they may come to the Lord with the peace, which in their letters to us the martyrs have desired to be given to them": *CSEL* 3², pp. 523-524; PL 4, 265; see *Epistle 19* (alias: 13), 2, CSEL 3², p. 525; *PL 4, 267.*

See Eusebius of Caesarea, *History of the Church* 1, 6. 42: CGS Eus. 2, 2, 610; *PG* 20, 614-615.

[29] See Ambrose, *On Penance 1, 15: ".* . . for he is cleansed by certain works of the whole people and is washed in the tears of the people, who is redeemed from sin by the prayers and weeping of the people and is cleansed in the inner man. For to his Church, which merited the coming of the Lord Jesus in order that all might be redeemed by one, Christ gave the power to redeem one by means of all": *PL 16,* 511.

[30] See Tertullian, *On Penance* 10, 5-6: "The body cannot rejoice when one of its members suffers, but the whole body must needs suffer with it and help to cure it. The Church is in both one and the other; the Church, however, is Christ. When therefore you cast yourself at the knees of your brothers, it is Christ whom you touch, it is Christ whom you implore. In like manner, when they shed tears for you, it is Christ who sorrows, Christ who supplicates the Father. And what the Son requests is always easily obtained": *CCL 1, p. 337; PL 1, 1356.*

See Augustine, *Exposition on Ps 85*, 1: *CCL* 39, pp. 1176-1177; *PL* 37, 1082.

[31] See *Acts 20, 28.* See also Council of Trent, Session XXIII, *Decree on the Sacrament of Orders,* ch. 4: D.S. 1768; 1 Vatican Council, Session IV, *Dogmatic Constitution on the Church..* ch. 3: D.S. 3061; 11 Vatican Council, *Dogmatic Constitution on the Church,* n. 20: A.A.S., *57 (1965), P.* 23.

See Ignatius of Antioch, To *the Church of Smyrna* 8, 1: "Apart from the Bishop, let no one perform any of the functions that pertain to the Church . . .": Funk, *The Apostolic Fathers 1,* p. 283.

the common good and suitable for fostering piety, to be performed by the penitents themselves and sometimes by others among the faithful. [32]

IV

7. The conviction existing in the Church that the pastors of the flock of the Lord could set the individual free from the vestiges of sins by applying the merits of Christ and of the saints led gradually, in the course of the centuries and under the influence of the Holy Spirit's continuous inspiration of the people of God, to the usage of indulgences which represented a progression in the doctrine and discipline of the Church rather than a change. [33] From the roots of revelation a new advantage grew in benefit to the faithful and the entire Church.

The use of indulgences, which spread gradually, became a very evident fact in the history of the Church when the Roman Pontiffs decreed that certain works useful to the common good of the Church "could replace all penitential practices" [34] and that the faithful who were "truly repentant and had confessed their sins" and performed such works were granted "by the mercy of Almighty God and . . . trusting in the merits and the authority of his Apostles" and "by virtue of the fullness of the apostolic power," not only full and abundant forgiveness, but the most complete forgiveness for their sins possible." [35]

---

[32] See Council of Nicaea I, can 12: ". . . those who by their reverence, tears, patience and good works show that in their conduct and disposition they have really been converted can, after having spent the required period of time as 'hearers,' be admitted to join the faithful in prayer, saving the right of the Bishop to treat them with greater leniency . . .": Mansi, *SS. Conciliorum collectio* 2, 674.

See Council of Neo-Caesarea, can. 3: l.c. 540.

See Innocent I, *Epistle* 25, 7, 10: PL 20, 559.

See Leo the Great, *Epistle* 159, 6: PL 54, 1138.

See Basil the Great, *Epistle* 217 (3rd canonical), 74: "Yet if any of those who have fallen into the above-mentioned sins should show himself earnest In doing penance, he who by God's mercy has been given the power to loose and to bind will not be deserving of censure if, because of the extraordinary penance already performed by the sinner, he should exercise clemency and shorten the time of the penance. For, what is narrated in the Scriptures teaches us that those who give themselves with greater intensity to penance quickly receive the mercy of God": *PG* 32, 803.

See Ambrose, *On Penance* 1, 15 (see note 29 above).
[33] See Vincent of Lerins, *Commonitorium primum* 23: PL 50, 667-668.
[34] See Council of Clermont, can. 2: "If anyone, moved solely by devotion to the exclusion of any desire for renown or riches, shall set out to liberate the Church of God in Jerusalem, that journey shall be accounted as satisfaction for every penance": Mansi, *SS. Conciliorum collectio* 20, 816.
[35] See Boniface VIII, Bull *Antiquorum habet*: "We have It on the trustworthy testimony of very early writers, that liberal remissions and indulgences for sins were granted to those who visited the venerable basilica of the Prince of the Apostles in Rome. We therefore, . . . holding these remissions and indulgences to be singly and collectively valid and pleasing, confirm and approve them by virtue of the Apostolic authority . . . . Trusting in the mercy of Almighty God and in the merits and authority of the same Apostles and after consultation with our brothers, We by virtue of the fullness of the Apostolic authority do now for this centennial year and will in the future for each recurring centennial year grant, not only a full and more abundant, but the fullest pardon of sins to those who, truly repentant and having confessed their sins, devoutly visit these basilicas . . . ": D.S. 868.

For "the only-begotten son of God . . . has won a treasure for the militant Church . . . and has entrusted it to blessed Peter, the keybearer of heaven, and to his successors, Christ's vicars on earth, that they may distribute it to the faithful for their salvation, applying it mercifully for reasonable causes to all who are repentant and have confessed their sins, at times remitting completely and at times partially the temporal punishment due sin in a general as well as in special ways insofar as they judge it to be fitting in the eyes of the Lord. It is known that the merits of the Blessed Mother of God and of all the elect . . . add further to this treasure." [36]

8. The remission of the temporal punishment due for sins already forgiven insofar as their guilt is concerned has been called specifically "indulgence." [37]

It has something in common with other ways or means of eliminating the vestiges of sin but at the same time it is clearly distinct from them.

In an indulgence in fact, the Church, making use of its power as minister of the Redemption of Christ, not only prays but by an authoritative intervention dispenses to the faithful suitably disposed the treasury of satisfaction which Christ and the saints won for the remission of temporal punishment. [38]

The aim pursued by ecclesiastical authority in granting indulgences is not only that of helping the faithful to expiate the punishment due sin but also that of urging them to perform works of piety, penitence and charity--particularly those which lead to growth in faith and which favor the common good. [39]

---

[36] Clement VI, Jubilee Bull Unigenitus Dei Filius: D.S. 1025, 1026, 1027,

[37] See Leo X, Decree *Cum postquam*: . . . "We have considered it our duty to make clear to you, that the Church of Rome, which all others are obliged to follow as their Mother, has traditionally taught, that the Roman Pontiff, as the successor of Peter the Bearer of the Keys and as the Vicar of Jesus Christ on earth, can for a reasonable cause grant from the superabundance of the merits of Christ and the Saints indulgences in favor of those of the faithful who, whether in this life or in purgatory, are members of Christ, joined to him in charity; this he can do by virtue of the power of the keys, the power namely to open the kingdom of heaven by freeing the faithful from impediments that bar them from it (from the impediment of guilt for their actual sins by the Sacrament of Penance and from the impediment of temporal punishment due in divine justice for these sins by ecclesiastical indulgence). It is also the tradition of this Church that, in granting by Apostolic authority an indulgence whether for the living or the dead, the Roman Pontiff dispenses the treasury of the merits of Christ and the Saints and that it was his wont to grant an indulgence (for the living) after the manner of an absolution and (for the dead) to transfer it in the form of a suffrage. Therefore all, both living and dead, who truly gain an indulgence, are freed from as much of the temporal punishment due in divine justice for their sins, as is granted by the indulgence acquired": D.S. 1447-1448.

[38] See Paul VI, Epistle *Sacrosancta Portiunculae*: "An indulgence, which the Church grants to the penitent, is a manifestation of that marvelous Communion of Saints, which by the single bond of the charity of Christ mystically unites the Most Blessed Virgin Mary and the company of the faithful, whether triumphant in heaven or detained in purgatory or still living as pilgrims upon earth. For an indulgence, given by the intervention of the Church, lessens or entirely remits the punishment, by which a person is in a certain sense prevented from attaining a closer union with God. The repentant, therefore, will find in this unique form of ecclesial charity ever available help in putting off the old man and putting on the new, 'who is being renewed unto perfect knowledge according to the image of his Creator' (*Col* 3, 10)": A.A.S., 58 (1966), pp. 633-634.

[39] See Paul VI, Epistle *Sacrosancta Portiunculae*: "As for those of the faithful who are repentant and strive to attain to this 'metanoia,' the Church comes to their help, for the reason that, having sinned, they now aspire to that holiness, with which they were clothed in Baptism. By grants of indulgences, she enfolds these her children in a maternal embrace, helping and sustaining them in their weakness and frailty. An indulgence, therefore, Is

And if the faithful offer indulgences in suffrage for the dead, they cultivate charity in an excellent way and while raising their minds to heaven, they bring a wiser order into the things of this world.

The Magisterium of the Church has defended and illustrated this doctrine in various documents. [40] Unfortunately, the practice of indulgences has at times been improperly used

---

not some easy way, by which we can escape the necessity of doing penance for sin. It is rather a support, which each of the faithful, humbly conscious of his weakness, finds in the mystical Body of Christ, 'collaborating in its entirety by charity, example and prayers to effect his conversion' *(Dogmatic Constitution on the Church, n. 11)"*: *A.A.S., 58 (1966). p. 632.*

[40] Clement VI, Jubilee Bull *Unigenitus Dei Filius:* D.S. 1026.

Clement VI, Epistle *Super quibusdam: D.S. 1059.*

Martin V, Bull *Inter cunctas:* D.S. 1266.

Sixtus IV, Bull *Salvator noster:* D.S. *139-8.*

Sixtus IV, Encyclical *Romani Pontificis provida:* "Desiring to counteract by Our Briefs. . . these scandals and errors, We have written to . . . prelates to notify the faithful, that the plenary indulgence for the souls in purgatory was granted by Us after the manner of a suffrage, not in order that the faithful might be deterred by this indulgence from performing pious and good works, but in order that the indulgence might be of salutary benefit to the souls (in purgatory) after the manner of a suffrage and profit them, just as would devout prayers and pious alms said and offered for the welfare of these souls. . . . It was not that We intended to say, nor do We now intend to say or wish to imply, that an indulgence is of no more benefit or value than alms or prayers or that alms and prayers are of equal benefit or value as an indulgence after the manner of suffrage; for, We know that there is a great difference between alms and prayers on the one hand and an indulgence after the manner of a suffrage on the other; but We said that an indulgence (after the manner of a suffrage) avails (the souls in purgatory) just as ('perinde acsi') do prayers and alms, that is, 'in the same manner.' And because prayers and alms have a suffrage-value when performed for the souls in purgatory, We, to whom the fullness of power has been given by God, desiring to assist the souls in purgatory with suffrages from the treasury of the universal Church - a treasury made up of the merits of Christ and the Saints and committed to Us-have granted the above-mentioned indulgence . . .": D.S. 1405-1406.

Leo X, *Bull Exsurge Domine: D.S. 1467-1472.*

Pius VI, Constitution *Auctorem fidei,* prop. *40:* "The proposition is false, rash, injurious to the merits of Christ, and long since condemned in article 19 of Luther, which asserts, 'that according to its precise meaning an indulgence is nothing more than the remission of part of that penance to which a sinner is obliged according to the stipulations of the canons,' as though an indulgence, apart from the, mere remission of a canonical penalty, does not also effect the remission of the temporal punishment due the divine justice for actual sins": D.S. 2640. *Ibid.,* prop. 41: "Likewise false, rash, injurious to the merits of Christ and the Saints, and long since condemned in article *17* of Luther is the statement subjoined to the above proposition, 'that the scholastics, puffed up by their subtleties, introduced an erroneous understanding of the treasury of the merits of Christ and the Saints and in place of the clear notion of absolution from a canonical penalty substituted the confused and false notion of applying these merits,' as though the treasures of the Church, on which the Pope draws in granting indulgences, were not the merits of Christ and the Saints": D.S. 2641. *Ibid.,* prop 42: "Likewise false, rash, offensive to pious ears, injurious to the Roman Pontiffs and to the practice and understanding of the universal Church, leading to the condemned heretical error of Peter of Osma, and condemned also in article 22 of Luther is the statement added to the above proposition, that it is still more to be regretted that it was decided to transfer this fanciful application (of merits) to the departed": D.S. 2642.

either through "untimely and superfluous indulgences" by which the power of the keys was humiliated and penitential satisfaction weakened, [41] or through the collection of "illicit profits" by which indulgences were blasphemously defamed. [42] But the Church, in deploring and correcting these improper uses "teaches and establishes that the use of indulgences must be preserved because it is supremely salutary for the Christian people and authoritatively approved by the sacred councils; and it condemns with anathema those who maintain the uselessness of indulgences or deny the power of the Church to grant them." [43]

9. The Church also in our days then invites all its sons to ponder and meditate well on how the use of indulgences benefits their lives and indeed all Christian society.

To recall briefly the most important considerations, this salutary practice teaches us in the first place how it is "sad and bitter to have abandoned . . . the Lord God." [44] Indeed the faithful when they acquire indulgences understand that by their own powers they could not remedy the harm they have done to themselves and to the entire community by their sin, and they are therefore stirred to a salutary humility.

Furthermore, the use of indulgences shows us how closely we are united to each other in Christ, and how the supernatural life of each can benefit others so that these also may be more easily and more closely united with the Father. Therefore the use of indulgences effectively influences charity in us and demonstrates that charity in an outstanding manner when we offer indulgences as assistance to our brothers who rest in Christ.

10. Likewise, the religious practice of indulgences reawakens trust and hope in a full reconciliation with God the Father, but in such a way as will not justify any negligence nor in any way diminish the effort to acquire the dispositions required for full communion with God. Although indulgences are in fact free gifts, nevertheless they are granted for the living as well as for the dead only on determined conditions. To acquire them, it is indeed required on the one hand that prescribed works be performed, and on the other that the faithful have the necessary dispositions, that is to say, that they love God, detest sin, place their trust in the merits of Christ and believe firmly in the great assistance they derive from the Communion of Saints.

In addition, it should not be forgotten that by acquiring indulgences the faithful submit docilely to the legitimate pastors of the Church and above all to the successor of Blessed

---

Pius XI, Proclamation of the Extraordinary Holy Year *Quod nuper:*" . . . We grant and impart mercifully in the Lord the fullest remission of the entire debt of punishment which they owe in atonement for their sins, provided they have first obtained the remission and pardon of the sins themselves": *A.A.S.*, 25 (1933), p. 8.

Pius XII, Proclamation of the Universal Jubilee Iubilaeum maximum: "To all the faithful who in the course of this year of atonement, having duly received the Sacraments of Penance and Holy Communion, devoutly visit the Basilicas and recite . . . prayers . . ., we grant and impart mercifully in the Lord the fullest remission of the entire debt of punishment which they owe in expiation for their sins": A.A.S., 41 (1949), pp. 258-259.

[41] See IV Lateran Council, ch. 62: D.S. 819.
[42] See Council of Trent, Decree on Indulgences: D.S. 1835.
[43] See n. 42.
[44] *Jer* 2, 19.

Peter, the keybearer of heaven, to whom the Savior himself entrusted the task of feeding his flock and governing his Church.

The salutary institution of indulgences therefore contributes in its own way to bringing it about that the Church appear before Christ without blemish or defect, but holy and immaculate, [45] admirably united with Christ in the supernatural bond of charity. Since in fact by means of indulgences members of the Church who are undergoing purification are united more speedily to those of the Church in heaven, the kingdom of Christ is through these same indulgences established more extensively and more speedily "until we all attain to the unity of the faith and of the deep knowledge of the Son of God, to perfect manhood, to the mature measure of the fullness of Christ." [46]

11. Therefore Holy Mother Church, supported by these truths, while again recommending to the faithful the practice of indulgences as something very dear to the Christian people during the course of many centuries and in our days as well --this is proven by experience--does not in any way intend to diminish the value of other means of sanctification and purification, first and foremost among which are the Sacrifice of the Mass and the Sacraments, particularly the Sacrament of Penance. Nor does it diminish the importance of those abundant aids which are called sacramentals or of the works of piety, penitence and charity. All these aids have this in common that they bring about sanctification and purification all the more efficaciously, the more closely the faithful are united with Christ the Head and the Body of the Church by charity. The preeminence of charity in the Christian life is confirmed also by indulgences. For indulgences cannot be acquired without a sincere conversion of mentality (metanoia) and unity with God, to which the performance of the prescribed works is added. Thus the order of charity is preserved, into which is incorporated the remission of punishment by distribution from the Church's treasury.

While recommending that its faithful not abandon or neglect the holy traditions of their forebears but welcome them religiously as a precious treasure of the Catholic family and duly esteem them, the Church nevertheless leaves it to each to use these means of purification and sanctification with the holy and free liberty of the sons of God. It constantly reminds them, though, of those things which are to be given preference because they are necessary or at least better and more efficacious for the attainment of salvation. [47]

Holy Mother Church has then deemed it fitting, in order to give greater dignity and esteem to the use of indulgences, to introduce some innovations into its discipline of indulgences and has accordingly ordered the issuance of new norms.

V

---

[45] See *Eph* 5, 27.
[46] See *Eph* 4, 13.
[47] See Thomas, *Commentary on 4th Book of Sentences*, dist. 20, q. 1, a. 3, q. la 2, ad 2 (*S. Th. Suppl.* q. 25, a. 2, ad 2): ". . . although such indulgences are of great value for the remission of temporal punishment, still other works of satisfaction are more meritorious from the standpoint of the essential reward; this is infinitely better than the remission of temporal punishment."

12. The following norms introduce appropriate variations in the discipline of indulgences, taking into consideration the proposals advanced by the episcopal conferences.

The rulings of the Code of Canon Law and of the decrees of the Holy See concerning indulgences which do not go counter to the new norms remain unchanged.

In drawing up the new norms these three considerations have been particularly observed: to establish a new measurement for partial indulgences; to reduce considerably the number of plenary indulgences; and, as for the so-called "real" and "local" indulgences, to reduce them and give them a simpler and more dignified formulation.

Regarding partial indulgences, with the abolishment of the former determination of days and years, a new norm or measurement has been established which takes into consideration the action itself of the faithful Christian who performs a work to which an indulgence is attached.

Since by their acts the faithful can obtain, in addition to the merit which is the principal fruit of the act, a further remission of temporal punishment in proportion to the degree that the charity of the one performing the act is greater, and in proportion to the degree that the act itself is performed in a more perfect way, it has been considered fitting that this remission of temporal punishment which the Christian faithful acquire through an action should serve as the measurement for the remission of punishment which the ecclesiastical authority bountifully adds by way of partial indulgence.

It has also been considered fitting to reduce appropriately the number of plenary indulgences in order that the faithful may hold them in greater esteem and may in fact acquire them with the proper dispositions. For indeed the greater the proliferation (of indulgences) the less is the attention given them; what is offered in abundance is not greatly appreciated. Besides, many of the faithful need considerable time to prepare themselves properly for acquisition of a plenary indulgence.

As regards the "real" and "local" indulgences, not only has their number been reduced considerably, but the designations themselves have been abolished to make it clearer that indulgences are attached to the actions performed by the faithful and not to objects or places which are but the occasion for the acquisition of the indulgences. In fact, members of pious associations can acquire the indulgences proper to their associations without the requirement of the use of distinctive objects.

Norms

N. 1. An indulgence is the remission before God of the temporal punishment due sins already forgiven as far as their guilt is concerned, which the follower of Christ with the proper dispositions and under certain determined conditions acquires through the intervention of the Church which, as minister of the Redemption, authoritatively dispenses and applies the treasury of the satisfaction won by Christ and the saints.

N. 2. An indulgence is partial or plenary according as it removes either part or all of the temporal punishment due sin.

N. 3. Partial as well as plenary indulgences can always be applied to the dead by way of suffrage.

N. 4. A partial indulgence will henceforth be designated only with the words "partial indulgence" without any determination of days or years.

N. 5. The faithful who at least with a contrite heart perform an action to which a partial indulgence is attached obtain, in addition to the remission of temporal punishment acquired by the action itself, an equal remission of punishment through the intervention of the Church.

N. 6. A plenary indulgence can be acquired only once a day, except for the provisions contained in No. 18 for those who are on the point of death. A partial indulgence can be acquired more than once a day, unless there is an explicit indication to the contrary.

N. 7. To acquire a plenary indulgence it is necessary to perform the work to which the indulgence is attached and to fulfill three conditions : sacramental confession, Eucharistic Communion and prayer for the intentions of the Supreme Pontiff. It is further required that all attachment to sin, even to venial sin, be absent.

If this disposition is in any way less than complete, or if the Prescribed three conditions are not fulfilled, the indulgence will only be partial, except for the provisions contained in No. 11 for those who are "impeded."

N. 8 The three conditions may be fulfilled several days before or after the performance of the prescribed work; nevertheless it is fitting that Communion be received and the prayers for the intentions of the Supreme Pontiff be said the same day the work is performed.

N. 9. A single sacramental confession suffices for gaining several plenary indulgences, but Communion must be received and prayers for the Supreme Pontiff's intentions recited for the gaining of each plenary indulgence.

N. 10. The condition of praying for the Supreme Pontiff's intentions is fully satisfied by reciting one Our Father and one Hail Mary; nevertheless the individual faithful are free to recite any other prayer according to their own piety and devotion toward the Supreme Pontiff.

N. 11. While there is no change in the faculty granted by canon 935 of the Code of Canon Law to confessors to commute for those who are "impeded" either the prescribed work itself or the required conditions [for the acquisition of indulgences], local Ordinaries can grant to the faithful over whom they exercise authority in accordance with the law, and who live in places where it is impossible or at least very difficult for them to receive the sacraments of confession and Communion, permission to acquire a plenary indulgence without confession and Communion provided they are sorry for their sins and have the intention of receiving these sacraments as soon as possible.

N. 12. The division of indulgences into "personal," "real" and "local" is abolished so as to make it clearer that indulgences are attached to the actions of the faithful even though at times they may be linked with some object or place.

N. 13. The Enchiridion of Indulgences is to be revised with a view to attaching indulgences only to the most important prayers and works of piety, charity and penance.

N. 14. The list and summaries of indulgences special to religious orders, congregations, societies of those living in community without vows, secular institutes and the pious associations of faithful are to be revised as soon as possible in such a way that plenary indulgences may be acquired only on particular days established by the Holy See acting on the recommendation of the Superior General, or in the case of pious associations, of the local Ordinary.

N. 15. A plenary indulgence applicable only to the dead can be acquired in all churches and public oratories -- and in semipublic oratories by those who have the right to use them --on November 2.

In addition, a plenary indulgence can be acquired twice a year in parish churches: on the feast of the church's titular saint and on August 2, when the "Portiuncula" occurs, or on some other more opportune day determined by the Ordinary.

All the indulgences mentioned above can be acquired either on the days established or--with the consent of the Ordinary--on the preceding or the following Sunday.

Other indulgences attached to churches and oratories are the to be revised as soon as possible.

N. 16. The work prescribed for acquiring a plenary indulgence connected with a church or oratory consists in a devout visit and the recitation of one Our Father and the Creed.

N. 17. The faithful who use with devotion an object, piety (crucifix, cross, rosary, scapular or medal) properly blessed by any priest, can acquire a partial indulgence.

But if this object of piety is blessed by the Supreme Pontiff or any bishop, the faithful who use it devoutly can also acquire a plenary indulgence on the feast of the holy Apostles Peter and Paul, provided they also make a profession of faith using any legitimate formula.

N. 18. To the faithful in danger of death who cannot be assisted by a priest to bring them the sacraments and impart the apostolic blessing with its attendant plenary indulgence (according to canon 468, 2 of the Code of Canon Law) Holy Mother Church nevertheless grants a plenary indulgence to be acquired at the point of death, provided they are properly disposed and have been in the habit of reciting some prayers during their lifetime. To use a crucifix or cross in connection with the acquisition of this plenary indulgence is a laudable practice.

This plenary indulgence at the point of death can be acquired by the faithful even if they have already obtained an indulgence on the same day.

N. 19. The norms established regarding plenary indulgences particularly those referred to in N. 6, apply also to what up to now have been known as the "toties quoties" ["as often as"] plenary indulgences.

No. 20. Holy Mother Church, extremely solicitous for faithful departed, has decided that suffrages be applied to them to the widest possible extent at any Sacrifice of the whatsoever, abolishing all special privileges in this regard.

Transitional Norms

These new norms regulating the acquisition of indulgences will become valid three months from the date of publication of this constitution in the Acta Apostolicae Sedis.

Indulgences attached to the use of objects of piety which are not mentioned above cease three months after the date of publication of this constitution in the Acta Apostolicae Sedis.

The revisions mentioned in N. 14 and N. 15 must be submitted to the Sacred Apostolic Penitentiary within a year. Two years after the date of this constitution, indulgences which have not been confirmed will become null and void.

We will that these statutes and prescriptions of ours be established now and remain in standing, if it is necessary so to state, the Apostolic Constitutions and Directives published by our Predecessors or any other prescriptions even if they might be worthy of special mention or should require particular repeal.

Given at Rome at St. Peter's on January 1, the octave of the Nativity of our Lord Jesus Christ, 1967, the fourth year of Our Pontificate.

Pope Paul VI

Supplement - More Indulgenced Prayers

Acts of the Theological Virtues and of Contrition
(See n.2, p.19)

Act of Faith

O my God, who are infallible Truth and can neither deceive nor be deceived, I firmly believe all that you have revealed and propose to my belief through your holy Church, because you have revealed it. I believe that you are one in nature and three in Persons: the Father, the Son, and the Holy Spirit. I believe that you are the Creator of all things and that you reward the just for all eternity in heaven and punish the wicked for all eternity in hell. I believe that Jesus Christ is the Son of God made man, that he suffered and died for my sins and rose from the dead in glory, and that it is only in him through the Holy Spirit that eternal life is given to men. I believe in fine all that your holy Church believes. I thank you for having called me to the true faith, and I protest that with the help of your grace I will live and die in this holy faith.

Act of Hope

O my God, trusting in your promises and because you are faithful, powerful and merciful, I hope, through the merits of Jesus Christ, for the pardon of my sins, final perseverance and the blessed glory of heaven.

Act of Love

O my God, because you are infinite goodness and worthy of infinite love, I love you with my whole heart above all things, and for love of you I love my fellow-men as myself.

Act of Contrition

O my God, I repent with my whole heart of all my sins, and I detest them, because I have deserved the loss of heaven and the pains of hell, but most of all because I have offended you, infinite Goodness. I firmly purpose with the help of your grace, which I pray you to grant me now and always, to do penance and rather to die than offend you again. I purpose also to receive the holy Sacraments during my life and at my death

An Act of Spiritual Communion
(See n.15, p. 23)

My Jesus, I believe that you are in the Blessed Sacrament. I love you above all things, and I long for you in my soul. Since I cannot now receive you sacramentally, come at least spiritually into my heart. As though you have already come, I embrace you and unite myself entirely to you; never permit me to be separated from you.

Litanies

(See n.29, p.28)

Litany of the Most Holy Name of Jesus

Lord, have mercy.

Christ, have mercy.

Lord, have mercy.

Jesus, hear us.

Jesus, graciously hear us.

God, the Father of Heaven,
    have mercy on us .

God the Son, Redeemer of the world,
    have mercy on us .

God, the Holy Spirit,
    have mercy on us .

Holy Trinity, one God,
    have mercy on us .

Jesus, Son of the living God,
    have mercy on us .

Jesus, Splendor of the Father,
    have mercy on us .

Jesus, Brightness of eternal Light,
    have mercy on us .

Jesus, King of Glory,
    have mercy on us .

Jesus, Sun of Justice,
    have mercy on us .

Jesus, Son of the Virgin Mary,
    have mercy on us .

Jesus, most amiable,
    have mercy on us .

Jesus, most admirable,
    have mercy on us .

Jesus, the mighty God,
    have mercy on us .

Jesus, Father of the world to come,
    have mercy on us .

Jesus, angel of great counsel,
    have mercy on us .

Jesus, most powerful,
    have mercy on us .

Jesus, most patient,
    have mercy on us .

Jesus, most obedient,
    have mercy on us .

Jesus, meek and humble of heart,
    have mercy on us .

Jesus, Lover of Chastity,
    have mercy on us .

Jesus, our Lover,
    have mercy on us .

Jesus, God of Peace,
    have mercy on us .

Jesus, Author of Life,
    have mercy on us .

Jesus, Model of Virtues,
    have mercy on us .

Jesus, zealous for souls,
    have mercy on us .

Jesus, our God,
    have mercy on us .

Jesus, our Refuge,
    have mercy on us .

Jesus, Father of the Poor,
    have mercy on us .

Jesus, Treasure of the Faithful,
    have mercy on us .

Jesus, good Shepherd,
    have mercy on us .

Jesus, true Light,
    have mercy on us .

Jesus, eternal Wisdom,
    have mercy on us .

Jesus, infinite Goodness,
    have mercy on us .

Jesus, our Way and our life,
    have mercy on us .

Jesus, joy of the Angels,
    have mercy on us .

Jesus, King of the Patriarchs,
    have mercy on us .

Jesus, Master of the Apostles,
    have mercy on us .

Jesus, Teacher of the Evangelists,
    have mercy on us .

Jesus, Strength of Martyrs,

have mercy on us .
Jesus, Light of Confessors,
 have mercy on us .
Jesus, Purity of Virgins,
 have mercy on us .
Jesus, Crown of all Saints,
 have mercy on us .
Be merciful, spare us, O Jesus!
Be merciful, graciously hear us, O Jesus!
From all evil,
 deliver us, O Jesus .
From all sin,
 deliver us, O Jesus .
From your wrath,
 deliver us, O Jesus .
From the snares of the devil,
 deliver us, O Jesus .
From the spirit of fornication,
 deliver us, O Jesus .
From everlasting death,
 deliver us, O Jesus .
From the neglect of your inspirations,
 deliver us, O Jesus .
Through the mystery of your holy
Incarnation,
 deliver us, O Jesus .
Through your Nativity,
 deliver us, O Jesus .
Through your Infancy,
 deliver us, O Jesus .
Through your most divine Life,
 deliver us, O Jesus .

Through your Labors,
 deliver us, O Jesus .
Through your Agony and Passion,
 deliver us, O Jesus .
Through your Cross and Dereliction,
 deliver us, O Jesus .
Through your Sufferings,
 deliver us, O Jesus .
Through your Death and Burial,
 deliver us, O Jesus .
Through your Resurrection,
 deliver us, O Jesus .
Through your Ascension,
 deliver us, O Jesus .
Through your Institution of the Most Holy
Eucharist,
 deliver us, O Jesus .
Through your Joys,
 deliver us, O Jesus .
Through your Glory,
 deliver us, O Jesus .
Lamb of God, who take away the sins of
the world,
 spare us, O Jesus!
Lamb of God, who take away the sins of
the world,
 graciously hear us, O Jesus!
Lamb of God, who take away the sins of
the world,
 have mercy on us, O Jesus!
Jesus, hear us.
Jcsus, graciously hear us.

Let us pray. O Lord Jesus Christ, you have said, "Ask and you shall receive; seek, and you shall find; knock, and it shall be opened to you"; mercifully attend to our supplications, and grant us the grace of your most divine love, that we may love you with all our hearts, and in all our words and actions, and never cease to praise you.

Make us, O Lord, to have a perpetual fear and love of your holy name, for you never fail to govern those whom you solidly establish in your love. You, who live and reign forever and ever. R. Amen.

Litany of the Most Sacred Heart of Jesus

Lord, have mercy.
Christ, have mercy.

Lord, have mercy.
Christ, hear us.

Christ, graciously hear us.
God, the Father of Heaven,
        have mercy on us.
God the Son, Redeemer of the world,
        have mercy on us.
God, the Holy Spirit,
        have mercy on us.
Holy Trinity, One God,
        have mercy on us.
Heart of Jesus, Son of the Eternal Father,
        have mercy on us
Heart of Jesus, formed by the Holy Spirit
in the womb of the Virgin Mother,
        have mercy on us
Heart of Jesus, substantially united to the
Word of God,
        have mercy on us
Heart of Jesus, of Infinite Majesty,
        have mercy on us
Heart of Jesus, Sacred Temple of God,
        have mercy on us
Heart of Jesus, Tabernacle of the Most
High,
        have mercy on us
Heart of Jesus, House of God and Gate of
Heaven,
        have mercy on us
Heart of Jesus, burning furnace of charity,
        have mercy on us
Heart of Jesus, abode of justice and love,
        have mercy on us
Heart of Jesus, full of goodness and love,
        have mercy on us
Heart of Jesus, abyss of all virtues,
        have mercy on us
Heart of Jesus, most worthy of all praise,
        have mercy on us
Heart of Jesus, king and center of all
hearts,
        have mercy on us
Heart of Jesus, in whom are all the
treasures of wisdom and knowledge,
        have mercy on us
Heart of Jesus, in whom dwells the fullness
of divinity,
        have mercy on us

Heart of Jesus, in whom the Father was
well pleased, Heart of Jesus, of whose
fullness we have all received,
        have mercy on us
Heart of Jesus, desire of the everlasting
hills,
        have mercy on us
Heart of Jesus, patient and most merciful,
Heart of Jesus, enriching all who invoke
you,
        have mercy on us
Heart of Jesus. fountain of life and
holiness,
        have mercy on us
Heart of Jesus, propitiation for our sins,
        have mercy on us
Heart of Jesus, loaded down with
opprobrium,
        have mercy on us
Heart of Jesus, bruised for our offenses,
        have mercy on us
Heart of Jesus, obedient to death,
        have mercy on us
Heart of Jesus, pierced with a lance,
        have mercy on us
Heart of Jesus, source of all consolation,
        have mercy on us
Heart of Jesus, our life and resurrection,
        have mercy on us
Heart of Jesus, our peace and
reconciliation,
        have mercy on us
Heart of Jesus, victim for our sins,
        have mercy on us
Heart of Jesus, salvation of those who trust
in you,
        have mercy on us
Heart of Jesus, hope of those who die in
you,
        have mercy on us
Heart of Jesus, delight of all the Saints,
        have mercy on us
Lamb of God, who take away the sins of
the world,
        spare us, O Lord.
Lamb of God, who take away the sins of
the world,

graciously hear us, O Lord.
Lamb of God, who take away the sins of the world,

have mercy on us.

V. Jesus, meek and humble of heart.
R. Make our hearts like to yours.

Let us pray. Almighty and eternal God, look upon the Heart of your most beloved Son and upon the praises and satisfaction which he offers you in the name of sinners; and to those who implore your mercy, in your great goodness, grant forgiveness in the name of the same Jesus Christ, your Son, who lives and reigns with you forever and ever. R. Amen.

Litany of the Most Precious Blood of Jesus [1]

Lord, have mercy.
Christ, have mercy.
Lord, have mercy.
Christ, hear us.
Christ, graciously hear us.
God, the Father of Heaven,
        have mercy on us.
God the Son, Redeemer of the world,
        have mercy on us.
God, the Holy Spirit,
        have mercy on us.
Holy Trinity, One God,
        have mercy on us.
Blood of Christ, only-begotten Son of the Eternal Father,
        save us.
Blood of Christ, Incarnate Word of God,
        save us.
Blood of Christ, of the New and Eternal Testament,
        save us.
Blood of Christ, falling upon the earth in the Agony,
        save us.
Blood of Christ, shed profusely in the Scourging,
        save us.

Blood of Christ, flowing forth in the Crowning with Thorns,
        save us.
Blood of Christ, poured out on the Cross,
        save us.
Blood of Christ, price of our salvation,
        save us.
Blood of Christ, without which there is no forgiveness,
        save us.
Blood of Christ, Eucharistic drink and refreshment of souls,
        save us.
Blood of Christ, stream of mercy,
        save us.
Blood of Christ, victor over demons,
        save us.
Blood of Christ, courage of Martyrs,
        save us.
Blood of Christ, strength of Confessors,
        save us.
Blood of Christ, bringing forth Virgins,
        save us.
Blood of Christ, help of those in peril,
        save us.
Blood of Christ, relief of the burdened,
        save us.
Blood of Christ, solace in sorrow,
        save us.

[1] S.R.C., Feb. 24, 1960; A.A.S., 52 (1960), p.412

65

Blood of Christ, hope of the penitent,
save us.
Blood of Christ, consolation of the
dying,
save us.
Blood of Christ, peace and tenderness of
hearts,
save us.
Blood of Christ, pledge of eternal life,
save us.
Blood of Christ, freeing souls from
purgatory,
save us.

Blood of Christ, most worthy of all glory
and honor,
save us.
Lamb of God, who take away the sins of
the world,
spare us, O Lord!.
Lamb of God, who take away the sins of
the world,
graciously hear us, O Lord!.
Lamb of God, who take away the sins of
the world,
have mercy on us.

V. You have redeemed us, O Lord, in your Blood.
R. And made us, for our God, a kingdom.

Let us pray. Almighty and eternal God, you have appointed your only-begotten Son the Redeemer of the world, and willed to be appeased by his Blood. Grant we beg of you, that we may worthily adore this price of our salvation, and through its power be safeguarded from the evils of the present life, so that we may rejoice in its fruits forever in heaven. Through the same Christ our Lord. R. Amen.

Litany of the Blessed Virgin Mary

Lord, have mercy.
Christ, have mercy.
Lord, have mercy.
Christ, hear us.
Christ, graciously hear us.
God, the Father of Heaven, have mercy on us.
God the Son, Redeemer of the world, have mercy on us.
God the Holy Spirit, have mercy on us.
Holy Trinity, One God, have mercy on us.
Holy Mary,
pray for us.
Holy Mother of God,
pray for us.
Holy Virgin of virgins,
pray for us.
Mother of Christ,
pray for us.
Mother of divine grace,
pray for us.

Mother most pure,
pray for us.
Mother most chaste,
pray for us.
Mother inviolate,
pray for us.
Mother undefiled,
pray for us.
Mother most amiable,
pray for us.
Mother most admirable,
pray for us.
Mother of good counsel,
pray for us.
Mother of our Creator,
pray for us.
Mother of our Savior,
pray for us.
Virgin most prudent,
pray for us.
Virgin most venerable,

pray for us.
Virgin most renowned,
　　pray for us.
Virgin most powerful,
　　pray for us.
Virgin most merciful,
　　pray for us.
Virgin most faithful,
　　pray for us.
Mirror of justice,
　　pray for us.
Seat of wisdom,
　　pray for us.
Cause of our joy,
　　pray for us.
Spiritual vessel,
　　pray for us.
Vessel of honor,
　　pray for us.
Singular vessel of devotion,
　　pray for us.
Mystical rose,
　　pray for us.
Tower of David,
　　pray for us.
Tower of ivory,
　　pray for us.
House of gold,
　　pray for us.
Ark of the covenant,
　　pray for us.
Gate of heaven,
　　pray for us.
Morning star,
　　pray for us.
Health of the sick,
　　pray for us.
Refuge of sinners,

pray for us.
Comforter of the afflicted,
Help of Christians,
　　pray for us.
Queen of Angels,
　　pray for us.
Queen of Patriarchs,
　　pray for us.
Queen of Prophets,
　　pray for us.
Queen of Apostles,
　　pray for us.
Queen of Martyrs,
　　pray for us.
Queen of Confessors,
　　pray for us.
Queen of Virgins,
　　pray for us.
Queen of all Saints,
　　pray for us.
Queen conceived without original sin,
　　pray for us.
Queen assumed into heaven,
　　pray for us.
Queen of the most holy Rosary,
　　pray for us.
Queen of Peace,
　　pray for us.
Lamb of God, who take away the sins of
the world,
　　spare us, O Lord!.
Lamb of God, who take away the sins of
the world,
　　graciously hear us, O Lord!
Lamb of God, who take away the sins of
the world,
　　have mercy on us.

V. Pray for us, O holy Mother of God.
R. That we may be made worthy of the promises of Christ.

Let us pray. Grant, we beg you, O Lord God, that we your servants, may enjoy lasting health of mind and body, and by the glorious intercession of the Blessed Mary, ever Virgin, be delivered from present sorrow and enter into the joy of eternal happiness. Through Christ our Lord. R. Amen.

During Advent

Let us pray. O God, you willed that, at the message of an angel, your Word should take flesh in the womb of the Blessed Virgin Mary; grant to your suppliant people, that we, who believe her to be truly the Mother of God, may be helped by her intercession with you. Through the same Christ our Lord. R. Amen.

From Christmas to the Purification

Let us pray. O God, by the fruitful virginity of Blessed Mary, you bestowed upon the human race the rewards of eternal salvation; grant, we beg you, that we may feel the power of her intercession, through whom we have been made worthy to receive the Author of life, our Lord Jesus Christ your Son. Who lives and reigns with you forever and ever. R. Amen.

During Paschaltime

Let us pray. O God, who by the Resurrection of your Son, our Lord Jesus Christ, granted joy to the whole world; grant, we beg you, that through the intercession of the Virgin Mary, his Mother, we may attain the joys of eternal life. Through the same Christ our Lord. RAmen.

Litany of St. Joseph

Lord, have mercy.
Christ, have mercy.
Lord, have mercy.
Christ, hear us.
Christ, graciously hear us.
God, the Father of Heaven, have mercy on us.
God the Son, Redeemer of the world, have mercy on us.
God the Holy Spirit, have mercy on us.
Holy Trinity, One God, have mercy on us.
Holy Mary,
    pray for us.
St. Joseph,
    pray for us.
Renowned offspring of David,
    pray for us.
Light of Patriarchs,
    pray for us.
Spouse of the Mother of God,
    pray for us.
Chaste guardian of the Virgin,
    pray for us.
Foster father of the Son of God,

    pray for us.
Diligent protector of Christ,
    pray for us.
Head of the Holy Family,
    pray for us.
Joseph most just,
    pray for us.
Joseph most chaste,
    pray for us.
Joseph most prudent,
    pray for us.
Joseph most strong,
    pray for us.
Joseph most obedient,
    pray for us.
Joseph most faithful,
    pray for us.
Mirror of patience,
    pray for us.
Lover of poverty,
    pray for us.
Model of artisans,
    pray for us.
Glory of home life,

68

pray for us.
Guardian of virgins,
pray for us.
Pillar of families,
pray for us.
Solace of the wretched,
pray for us.
Hope of the sick,
pray for us.
Patron of the dying,
pray for us.
Terror of demons,

pray for us.
Protector of Holy Church,
pray for us.
Lamb of God, who take away the sins of
the world,
spare us, O Lord!.
Lamb of God, who take away the sins of
the world,
graciously hear us, O Lord!.
Lamb of God, who take away the sins of
the world,
have mercy on us. .

V. He made him the lord of his household.
R. And prince over all his possessions.

Let us pray. O God, in your ineffable providence you were pleased to choose Blessed Joseph
to be the spouse of your most holy Mother; grant, we beg you, that we may be worthy to have
him for our intercessor in heaven whom on earth we venerate as our Protector: You who live
and reign forever and ever. R. Amen.

Litany of the Saints

Lord, have mercy.
Christ, have mercy.
Lord, have mercy.
Christ, hear us.
Christ, graciously hear us.
God the Father of Heaven,
have mercy on us.
God the Son, Redeemer of the world,
have mercy on us.
God the Holy Spirit,
have mercy on us.
Holy Trinity, one God,
have mercy on us.
Holy Mary,
pray for us.
Holy Mother of God,
pray for us.
Holy Virgin of virgins,
pray for us.
St. Michael,
pray for us.
St. Gabriel,
pray for us.
St. Raphael,

pray for us.
All you holy Angels and Archangels,
pray for us.
All you holy orders of blessed Spirits,
pray for us.
St. John the Baptist,
pray for us.
St. Joseph,
pray for us.
All you holy Patriarchs and Prophets,
pray for us.
St. Peter,
pray for us.
St. Paul,
pray for us.
St. Andrew,
pray for us.
St. James,
pray for us.
St. John,
pray for us.
St. Thomas,
pray for us.
St. James,

pray for us.
St. Philip,
        pray for us.
St. Bartholomew,
        pray for us.
St. Matthew,
        pray for us.
St. Simon,
        pray for us.
St. Thaddeus,
        pray for us.
St. Matthias,
        pray for us.
St. Barnabas,
        pray for us.
St. Luke,
        pray for us.
St. Mark,
        pray for us.
All you holy Apostles and Evangelists,
        pray for us.
All you holy Disciples of the Lord,
        pray for us.
All you holy Innocents,
        pray for us.
St. Stephen,
        pray for us.
St. Lawrence,
        pray for us.
St. Vincent,
        pray for us.
Sts. Fabian and Sebastian,
        pray for us.
Sts. John and Paul,
        pray for us.
Sts. Cosmas and Damian,
        pray for us.
Sts. Gervase and Protase,
        pray for us.
All you holy Martyrs,
        pray for us.
St. Sylvester,
        pray for us.
St. Gregory,
        pray for us.
St. Ambrose,
        pray for us.

St. Augustine,
        pray for us.
St. Jerome,
        pray for us.
St. Martin,
        pray for us.
St. Nicholas,
        pray for us.
All you holy Bishops and Confessors,
        pray for us.
All you holy Doctors,
        pray for us.
St. Anthony,
        pray for us.
St. Benedict,
        pray for us.
St. Bernard,
        pray for us.
St. Dominic,
        pray for us.
St. Francis,
        pray for us.
All you holy Priests and Levites,
        pray for us.
All you holy Monks and Hermits,
        pray for us.
St. Mary Magdalen,
        pray for us.
St. Agatha,
        pray for us.
St. Lucy,
        pray for us.
St. Agnes,
        pray for us.
St. Cecilia,
        pray for us.
St. Catherine,
        pray for us.
St. Anastasia,
        pray for us.
All you holy Virgins and Widows,
        pray for us.
All you Holy Men and Women, Saints of
God,
make intercession for us.
        Be merciful,
spare us, O Lord.

Be merciful,
graciously hear us, O Lord.
From all evil, O Lord,
    deliver us.
From all sin,
    deliver us.
From your wrath,
    deliver us.
From sudden and unprovided death,
    deliver us.
From the snares of the devil,
    deliver us.
From anger, and hatred, and all ill-will,
    deliver us.
From the spirit of fornication,
    deliver us.
From lightning and tempest,
    deliver us.
From the scourge of earthquake,
    deliver us.
From plague, famine and war,
    deliver us.
From everlasting death,
    deliver us.
Through the mystery of your holy
Incarnation,
    deliver us.
Through your Coming,
    deliver us.
Through your Nativity,
    deliver us.
Through your Baptism and holy Fasting,
    deliver us.
Through your Cross and Passion,
    deliver us.
Through your Death and Burial,
    deliver us.
Through your holy Resurrection,
    deliver us.
Through your admirable Ascension,
    deliver us.
Through the coming of the Holy Spirit, the
Paraclete,
In the day of judgment,
    deliver us.
We sinners,
    we beseech you, hear us.

That you would spare us,
    we beseech you, hear us.
That you would pardon us,
    we beseech you, hear us.
That you would bring us to true penance,
    we beseech you, hear us.
That you would deign to govern and
preserve your holy Church,
    we beseech you, hear us.
That you would deign to preserve our
Apostolic Prelate, and all orders of the
Church in holy religion,
    we beseech you, hear us.
That you would deign to humble the
enemies of Holy Church,
    we beseech you, hear us.
That you would deign to give peace and
true concord to Christian kings and
princes,
    we beseech you, hear us.
That you would deign to grant peace and
unity to all Christian people,
    we beseech you, hear us.
That you would deign to call back to the
unity of the Church all who have strayed
from the truth and lead all unbelievers to
the light of the Gospel,
    we beseech you, hear us.
That you would deign to confirm and
preserve us in your holy service,
    we beseech you, hear us.
That you would lift up our minds to
heavenly desires,
    we beseech you, hear us.
That you would render eternal blessings to
all our benefactors,
    we beseech you, hear us.
That you would deliver our souls and the
souls of our brethren, relations and
benefactors, from eternal damnation,
    we beseech you, hear us.
That you would deign to give and preserve
the fruits of the earth,
    we beseech you, hear us.
That you would deign to grant eternal rest
to all the faithful departed,
    we beseech you, hear us.

That you would deign graciously to hear us,
    we beseech you, hear us.
Son of God,
    we beseech you, hear us.
Lamb of God, who take away the sins of the world,
spare us, O Lord. .
Lamb of God, who take away the sins of the world,
graciously hear us, O Lord. .
Lamb of God, who take away the sins of the world,
have mercy on us. .
Christ, hear us.
Christ, graciously hear us.
Lord, have mercy.
Christ, have mercy.
Lord, have mercy.

Our Father, etc. (inaudibly.

V. And lead us not into temptation.
R. But deliver us from evil.

[psalm 69]

Deign, O Lord, to rescue me;
O Lord, make haste to help me
Let them be put to shame and confounded
    who seek my life.
Let them be turned back in disgrace who
    desire my ruin.
Let them retire in their shame who say to
    me, "Aha, aha!"
But may all who seek you exult and be
    glad in you,
And may those who love your salvation
    say ever, "God be glorified!"
But I am afflicted and poor;
O God, hasten to me!
You are my help and my deliverer;
O Lord, hold not back!
Glory be to the Father, and to the Son, and
    to the Holy Spirit.

As it was in the beginning, is now, and
    ever shall be, world without end.
    Amen.

V. Save your servants.
R. Who trust in you, O my God.

V. Be a tower of strength for us, O Lord,
R. Against the attack of the enemy.

V. Let not the enemy prevail against us.
R. And let not the son of evil dare to harm us.

V. O Lord, deal not with us according to our sins.
N. Neither requite us according to our iniquities.

V. Let us pray for our Sovereign Pontiff N.
R. The Lord preserve him, and give him life, and make him blessed upon the earth, and deliver him not up to the will of his enemies.

V. Let us pray for our benefactors.
R. Deign, O Lord, for Your name's sake, to reward with eternal life all those who do us good. Amen.

V. Let us pray for the faithful departed.
R. Eternal rest give to them, O Lord; and let perpetual light shine upon them.

V. May they rest in peace.
R. Amen.

V. For our absent brethren.
R. Save your servants, who trust in you, my God.

V. Send them help, O Lord, from your sanctuary.
R. And sustain them from Zion.

V. O Lord, hear my prayer.
R. And let my cry come to you.

V. The Lord be with you.

Let us pray. O God, whose property is always to have mercy and to spare, receive our petition, that we, and all your servants who are bound by the chains of sin, may, by the compassion of your goodness, be mercifully absolved.

Graciously hear, we beg you, O Lord, the prayers of your suppliants, and pardon the sins of those who confess to you, that in your bounty you may grant us both pardon and peace.

In your clemency, O Lord, show us your ineffable mercy, that you may both free us from all our sins, and deliver us from the punishments which we deserve for them.

O God, who by sin are offended and by penance pacified, mercifully regard the prayers of your suppliant people, and turn away the scourges of your anger, which we deserve for our sins.

Almighty, everlasting God, have mercy upon your servant N., our Sovereign Pontiff, and direct him according to your clemency into the way of everlasting salvation, that by your grace he may desire those things that are pleasing to you, and perform them with all his strength.

O God, from whom are holy desires, good counsels, and just works, give to your servants that peace which the world cannot give, that our hearts be set to keep your commandments, and that, being removed from the fear of our enemies, we may pass our time in peace under your protection.

Burn our desires and our hearts with the fire of the Holy Spirit, O Lord, that we may serve you with a chaste body, and with a clean heart be pleasing to you.

O God, the Creator and Redeemer of all the faithful, grant to the souls of your servants and handmaids the remission of all their sins, that, through devout prayers, they may obtain the pardon which they always desired.

Direct, we beg you, O Lord, our actions by your holy inspirations, and carry them on by your gracious assistance, that every prayer and work of ours may begin always with you, and through you be happily ended.

Almighty and everlasting God, you have dominion over the living and the dead, and you are merciful to all who you foreknow will be yours by faith and good works; we humbly beg you that those for whom we intend to pour forth our prayers, whether this present world still detain them in the flesh, or the world to come has already received them out of their bodies, may, through the intercession of all your Saints, by the clemency of your goodness, obtain the remission of all their sins. Through Christ our Lord. R. Amen.

V. O Lord, hear my prayer.

R. And let my cry come to you.

V. May the almighty and merciful Lord graciously hear us. R. Amen.
V. And may the souls of the faithful departed, through the mercy of God, rest in peace. R. Amen.

Prayer for Sacerdotal or Religious Vocations

O Lord, send workers for your harvest, so that the commands of your only-begotten Son may always be obeyed and his sacrifice be everywhere renewed.

Look with favor upon your family, and ever increase its numbers. Enable it to lead its sons [daughters] to the holiness to which they are called and to work for the salvation of others. Through Christ our Lord. R. Amen.

The Mysteries of the Rosary

The Joyful Mysteries

1. The Annunciation of the Archangel Gabriel to the Virgin Mary
2. The Visitation of the Virgin Mary to the Parents of St. John the Baptist
3. The Birth of Our Lord at Bethlehem
4. The Presentation of Our Lord in the Temple
5. The Finding of Our Lord in the Temple

The Sorrowful Mysteries

1. The Agony of Our Lord in the Garden of Gethsemane
2. The Scourging of Our Lord at the Pillar
3. The Crowning of Our Lord with Thorns
4. The Carrying of the Cross by Our Lord to Calvary
5. The Crucifixion and Death of Our Lord

The Glorious Mysteries

1. The Resurrection of Our Lord from the dead
2. The Ascension of Our Lord into Heaven
3. The Descent of the Holy Spirit upon the Apostles
4. The Assumption of Our Blessed Lady into Heaven
5. The Coronation of Our Blessed Lady as Queen of Heaven and Earth

The Stations of the Cross

1. Jesus is condemned to death
2. Jesus bears his cross
3. Jesus falls the first time
4. Jesus meets his mother

5. Jesus is helped by Simon
6. Veronica wipes the face of Jesus
7. Jesus falls a second time
8. Jesus speaks to the women
9. Jesus falls a third time
10. Jesus is stripped of his garments
11. Jesus is nailed to the Cross
12. Jesus dies on the Cross
13. Jesus is taken down from the Cross
14. Jesus is placed in the tomb

Renewal of Baptismal Promises

I, N. N., who through the tender mercy of the Eternal Father was privileged to be baptized "in the name of the Lord Jesus" (Acts 19, 5) and thus to share in the dignity of his divine Sonship, wish now in the presence of this same loving Father and of his only-begotten Son to renew in all sincerity the promises I solemnly made at the time of my holy Baptism.

I, therefore, now do once again renounce Satan; I renounce all his works; I renounce all his allurements.

I believe in God, the Father almighty, Creator of heaven and earth. I believe in Jesus Christ, his only Son, our Lord, who was born into this world and who suffered and died for my sins and rose again. I believe in the Holy Spirit, the Holy Catholic Church, the communion of Saints, the forgiveness of sins, the resurrection of the body and life everlasting.

Having been buried with Christ unto death and raised up with him unto a new life, I promise to live no longer for myself or for that world which is the enemy of God but for him who died for me and rose again, serving God, my heavenly Father, faithfully and unto death in the holy Catholic Church.

Taught by our Savior's command and formed by the word of God, I now dare to say:

Our Father, who art in heaven, hallowed be thy name; thy kingdom come; thy will be done on earth as it is in heaven. Give us this day our daily bread; and forgive us our trespasses as we forgive those who trespass against us; and lead us not into temptation, but deliver us from evil. Amen.

*****

Printed in Dunstable, United Kingdom

66785454R00045